A PHOTOGRAPHIC GUIDE TO

BIRDS

OF SOUTHERN AFRICA

IAN SINCLAIR

D1409464

To my daughter, Kiera

Struik Publishers
(a division of New Holland Publishing (South Africa) (Pty) Ltd)
Cornelis Struik House
80 McKenzie Street, Cape Town 8001

New Holland Publishing is a member of
Johnnic Communications Ltd.
Visit us at **www.struik.co.za**

www.imagesofafrica.co.za

IMAGES OF AFRICA
PHOTO LIBRARY

First published in 1990
Second edition 1999
Third edition (new cover only) 2000
Fourth edition 2004
10 9 8 7 6 5 4 3 2

Concept design by Jenny Camons
Page design and artwork by Tracey Carstens
Typesetting by McManus Bros (Pty) Ltd, Cape Town
Reproduction by Fotoplate (Pty) Ltd, Cape Town
Printed and bound by Times Offset (M) Sdn Bhd, Malaysia

Front cover photograph: African Purple Swamphen (Nigel
Dennis /SIL)
Title page photograph: White Pelican (H. von Hörsten)
Back cover photograph: Cape Sugarbird (Nigel Dennis/SIL)
ISBN 1 77007 083 4

CONTENTS

INTRODUCTION

In the past few years bird-watching, or 'birding' as it is now commonly referred to, has become one of the fastest developing pastimes throughout the western world. To accommodate this rapid development, a wide range of books has become available, covering most aspects of the topic but with field guides predominating. So why then yet another guide to birds?

In the area that comprises the ornithological region of southern Africa (that is, the area south of the Zambezi and Cunene Rivers), nearly 900 species of birds are known to occur. However, as almost two-thirds of the species in this area are not common, have specialized habitat requirements, are extremely furtive and are thus difficult to find, or are virtually impossible to identify correctly unless one has years of experience, it is highly unlikely that one would see all these species. Many other species are only vagrants and have occurred fewer than five times and the chances of seeing these are remote. This leaves only a few hundred species that are seen frequently by the casual or novice birder.

This book has been designed with this in mind: the 260 species selected are not necessarily the most common in southern Africa but they are the conspicuous birds and thus likely to be encountered most frequently. These are the birds that you can expect to see on a day trip to the coast, or in a nature or game reserve. By using this book in the field you should be able to identify the bird you have seen or be able to deduce to which family the bird belongs and then later to identify the bird at home, using more comprehensive books.

One of the main attractions of birding is that birds are a highly visual and appealing subject and they occur in virtually all habitats. Although most birds are very visible and many are abundant, it is not always that easy to identify them correctly. Familiarize yourself with the different species that appear in the plates by leafing through the book when you have a spare moment so that you will be able to recognize a species the first time you see it in the wild. Most of the birds in the book are easily recognizable in the wild but there are a few that require more skill to identify.

Frequently a bird is not clearly seen, is seen only for a short period, or a feature on the bird may become exaggerated, possibly resulting in a misidentification. Avoid snap identifications: rather aim for sustained and better viewing to identify the bird. When confronted with a bird that is not instantly recognizable, first judge its size, then try to work out its general shape, colour pattern, the length of its tail, shape of its wings and every other detail which might be conspicuous. Often there is one striking feature that is sufficient to distinguish the bird, but sometimes it takes the combination of several features to make a positive identification.

In theory, the most satisfactory way to be certain of an identification is to photograph the bird and then, at your leisure, identify the bird from the photograph by consulting books or by showing the photograph to an expert. This may sound feasible but, in practice, the prohibitive costs of photographic equipment notwithstanding, taking the photograph requires a considerable amount of skill. A far better idea is to use a notebook and pencil and to jot down details of the bird you are watching and to make a rudimentary sketch showing the obvious features. From your notes and sketches the bird should be relatively easy to identify at a later stage.

Much has been written about the equipment necessary for birding and many of the books listed in the section of Further Reading contain sufficient detail to help you decide which binoculars, telescope, tape recorder and so on will best suit your purposes. There is also a book which suggests where and when to go birding in southern Africa. Many courses on bird identification are offered by different clubs, societies and universities and these will all help to hone your skills in the field. There is, however, no substitute for first hand observation and the longer you spend in the field improving your abilities in the correct identification of birds, the greater will be your understanding of birds in general.

HOW TO USE THIS BOOK

This book has been designed with clarity and ease of use in mind. The species' descriptions are succinct, with key identification pointers emphasized in italic type. Where necessary, photographs show both male and female to highlight plumage differences, and illustrate breeding and non-breeding dress, as well as adult and immature birds. The length of the bird (from bill tip to outstretched tail) is given, except in the case of the Ostrich whose measurement indicates its height. The call is mentioned only if it is characteristic of the bird. In each case, an up-to-date map has been provided to reflect the known distribution of the species. Birds that are similar in size, shape and colour – and are thus likely to be confused – are grouped for purposes of comparison. The thumbnail silhouettes are intended to guide you to the family of birds most closely resembling the bird you have seen, as you flick through the book.

A habitat map showing the various vegetation zones mentioned in the text, a glossary of birding terms, as well as a diagram showing the parts of a bird, are featured on pages 140 and 141.

ABBREVIATIONS AND SYMBOLS USED IN THIS BOOK

ad. = adult
imm. = immature
br. = breeding
non-br. = non-breeding
♂ = male   ♀ = female
S. = Southern

Common Ostrich *Struthio camelus* **Height 2 m**

Male

 Unmistakable: the *tallest and largest* bird in the region. The male has contrasting black and white plumage, a rufous tail, and a reddish front to the legs when breeding. The female and imm. are drab brown and white. Very young bird might be mistaken for a korhaan but has flattened bill, thick legs and is fluffy in appearance. Outside game reserves most birds are either domesticated or feral. A nocturnal loud booming is the call given by the male. Found in extreme desert conditions, open plains and bushveld.

African Penguin *Spheniscus demersus* **60-70 cm**

Adult   **Immature**

 The *black and white face pattern* on this small penguin is diagnostic. The general *upright stance* and black and white plumage render it unmistakable when seen ashore. At sea it swims very low in the water with only the neck and head breaking the surface. Imm. is a dark greyish-blue and lacks the head pattern of the ad. When travelling fast through water, it 'porpoises' at regular intervals. The loud, donkey-like braying call is given mostly at night. Most common on the south and west coasts where it breeds on offshore islands.

Little Grebe *Tachybaptus ruficollis* **23-29 cm**

Breeding

Non-breeding

One of the *smallest aquatic birds* in the region. *Sides of head are chestnut* during breeding season (diagnostic). Non-breeding birds are drab greyish-brown; in all plumages, a pale spot at the base of the bill is diagnostic. In flight the Little Grebe has very rapid wing beats and shows a white wing stripe and a bright white belly. Frequently dives; often will emerge with just the head showing to watch intruder. Call is a high-pitched, whinnying trill. Frequents freshwater areas with emergent vegetation.

Black-browed Albatross *Thalassarche melanophris* **81-95 cm**

Adult resembles a large Kelp Gull with much longer, straighter wings. Ad. has *white underwing with very broad black borders* and this, combined with a yellowish, orange-tipped bill, is diagnostic. Imm. has predominantly *dark underwing with a grey, black-tipped bill*, smoky smudges on head and an incomplete greyish collar. Sometimes ventures close inshore along the southern and western Cape coasts.

Adult

Sub-adult

7

Atlantic Yellow-nosed Albatross *Thalassarche chlororhynchos* 72-80 cm

Adult

Immature

Smaller and more slender than Black-browed Albatross and has *white underwing narrowly bordered with black*. The bill appears totally black but at close range a *yellow stripe is evident on the upper ridge*. Differs from Indian Yellow-nosed Albatross by having grey, not grey-cheeked white head. Imm. lacks yellow on bill. Frequently seen in colder waters of western Cape.

Pintado Petrel *Daption capense* 38-40 cm

An easily identifiable, conspicuous seabird. The *chequered black and white upperparts* are diagnostic; the underparts are predominantly white with a dark throat. Flight very floppy for a seabird but, in stronger winds, it glides and turns, twisting from side to side. Does not venture close to shore except during storms but is common around fishing boats.

White-chinned Petrel *Procellaria aequinoctialis* **51-58 cm**

J.C. SINCLAIR

Considerably larger than Sooty Shearwater, is much *darker brown, appearing almost black*, and lacks silvery underwing. Diagnostic *pale bill and white chin* can be seen at close range. Wings long and narrow; has a towering, careening flight action high above waves. Regularly ventures close inshore around the coast and frequently follows fishing trawlers. Normally silent but will utter a fast 'tititit' when alarmed.

A. WILSON

Sooty Shearwater *Puffinus griseus* **40-46 cm**

J.C. SINCLAIR

Smaller and paler than White-chinned Petrel and has diagnostic *silvery underwing*. Flight is swift and direct with rapid wing beats interspersed with glides when bird banks over waves and flashes its silvery underwings. On migration, very large concentrations of these birds come close inshore along the western Cape coast. They feed in mixed flocks with Cape Gannets and Cape Cormorants.

Antarctic Prion   *Pachyptila desolata*   **25-28 cm**

Prions are notoriously difficult to identify in the field but this is the prion most commonly encountered around the coast. Features common to all prions are the blue-grey upperparts with an open 'W' across the back and wings, a dark-tipped tail and white underparts. Sometimes occurs in large numbers; in adverse weather many are beach wrecked.

Great White Pelican   *Pelecanus onocrotalus*   **140-178 cm**

Adult

Immature

This large bird can be confused only with the smaller Pink-backed Pelican but the ad. is much *whiter and has contrasting black flight feathers and a brighter yellow pouch*. Imm. is much larger and a darker brown than imm. Pink-backed Pelican. Frequently flies in 'V' formation. Groups feed by herding shoals of fish and then scooping them up in their large bills. The only pelican in the Cape coastal area.

Pink-backed Pelican   *Pelecanus rufescens*   135-152 cm

A. WEAVING

 Noticeably *smaller than White Pelican* and much *drabber grey*; never as crisply white. The flight feathers do not contrast strongly with greyish wings and body and in flight *underwings appear uniform* in colour. The bill pouch is grey or pink, not yellow as in White Pelican. Imm. darker than ad. but never as dark brown as imm. White Pelican. More inclined to feed solitarily than White Pelican. Occurrence virtually restricted to KwaZulu-Natal coastal estuaries and freshwater lakes.

Cape Gannet   *Morus capensis*   87-100 cm

 Differs from the large albatrosses by being whiter, having a long, dagger-shaped bill and a long, pointed tail. Imm. is dark brown version of ad. and differs from White-chinned Petrel by fine speckling on back, its pale belly and much larger size. When feeding, plunges into sea from considerable height with partly folded wings. Seen regularly from shore in all weathers, sometimes as it gathers in large feeding flocks.

G. CUBITT

P.R.B. STEYN

Above: adult
Right: immature

11

White-breasted Cormorant *Phalacrocorax lucidus* **80-100 cm**

Adult   **Immature**

By far the largest of the cormorants. Has a clear white breast and throat and, in the breeding season, white thigh patches. Imm. has variable amount of white on breast and belly and is best distinguished from Reed Cormorant by its much larger size. Differs from similarly sized African Darter by having a much thicker neck, broader head and shorter tail. Coastal birds avoid feeding over the open ocean, preferring sheltered bays and estuaries.

Cape Cormorant *Phalacrocorax capensis* **61-65 cm**

Adult   **Immature**

The *most abundant marine cormorant* of the region. Sometimes vast numbers can be seen from the shore as they fly in straight lines or skeins to and from their feeding areas. Ad. is a glossy, bluish black with a conspicuous orange throat patch. Imm. is a dowdy brownish colour and lacks the white underparts of the larger White-breasted Cormorant. Feeds actively on anchovy and sardine shoals, leap-frogging over each other in pursuit of food.

Reed Cormorant   *Phalacrocorax africanus* **50-55 cm**

Adult

Immature

Most often seen with White-breasted Cormorant and Darter from which it is distinguished by being much smaller. Ad. in breeding plumage has a barred back, *orange face and throat*, and a *small erectile crest*. The *tail is proportionally longer and more graduated* than that of White-breasted Cormorant. Imm. is brownish-grey with white underparts. Often seen perched with wings outstretched on a prominent post over water. Occurs on large river systems and in freshwater habitats.

African Darter   *Anhinga rufa* **80 cm**

Adult

Immature

Resembles a cormorant but has a *thin, almost snake-like head and neck, and a long, stiletto-shaped bill*. The sides of the head and neck are rufous and the mantle and wing coverts are streaked with buff. When swimming, the body is held submerged with only the neck and head showing; the neck is held curved and moves backwards and forwards as the bird swims. Imm. has a white head which darkens with age. Found on dams and rivers.

13

Grey Heron   *Ardea cinerea* **90-100 cm**

A. WILSON

Adult

A. WILSON

Immature

A large, long-legged grey bird, often seen standing motionless in water while fishing. Closer inspection reveals a *yellow, dagger-shaped bill and a white head with black eye-stripe which ends in a wispy crest.* Imm. lacks black eye-stripe and crest, and is duller in colour. In flight can be distinguished from Black-headed Heron by having a uniform grey underwing. Mostly solitary except when breeding. It flies with the head and neck tucked tightly into the shoulders. Occurs widely in salt- and freshwater habitats.

Black-headed Heron   *Ardea melanocephala* **84-92 cm**

H. VON HÖRSTEN

Adult

G. CUBITT

Immature

The *black top of the head and hind neck contrast with the white throat* and render this heron unmistakable. Imm. has the black on the head and neck replaced with grey and could be confused with imm. Grey Heron but, like the ad., it has *contrasting black and white underwings.* Not normally associated with water, preferring to forage over grasslands; is attracted to burnt veld.

Little Egret *Egretta garzetta* 56-65 cm

A. WEAVING

A small white 'heron' with a black bill and diagnostic yellow toes. Habitually frequents shallows in freshwater and estuary areas where it feeds by dashing to and fro, repeatedly stabbing at its prey. During this frenzied feeding activity the yellow toes can often easily be seen. In breeding plumage shows wispy white head plumes and lace-like aigrettes on the lower back. Occurs in most freshwater habitats, at coastal estuaries, and at intertidal pools on rocky coasts.

Cattle Egret *Bubulcus ibis* 50-56 cm

H. VON HORSTEN

G. CUBITT

Breeding   **Non-breeding**

The white 'heron' seen following cattle or game. The breeding bird has a buffy crown, breast and back, and reddish legs; the non-breeding and imm. birds are white with brownish or greenish legs. Smaller than other white 'herons', and the most gregarious away from breeding colonies, often forming *flocks which follow cattle. They fly to their roosts in tight 'V' formations.*

Hamerkop   *Scopus umbretta*   48-56 cm

L. HES

The hammer-shaped profile of this bird's head and bill render it unmistakable. It is a brownish bird with long legs, a large black bill and a shaggy crest. The tail is finely barred. In flight, the bird might be mistaken for a bird of prey were it not for its long bill and the legs projecting beyond the tail. Normally associated with water where it wades in the shallows, searching for frogs, but it also patrols roadways in the morning, looking for amphibian road kills.

White Stork   *Ciconia ciconia*   102-120 cm

G. CUBITT

A large, *white, heron-like bird with contrasting black flight feathers and a bright red bill*. Legs are also bright red but become covered in excrement and appear greyish-white. Imm. similar to ad. except its bill and legs are duller red and the white plumage is dusted with brown. Congregates to feed, sometimes in large flocks; is particularly fond of lucerne. On hot days is often seen riding thermals in the company of vultures.

Abdim's Stork   *Ciconia abdimii*   **76-81 cm**

A. WILSON

 A black and white stork, considerably smaller than the White Stork with which it often associates. Distinguished from all other similar storks by its diagnostic white lower back. At close range, the blue face and greyish legs with red joints are noticeable. Often occurs in very large flocks in agricultural lands. Migrant; more abundant in some years than in others.

Marabou Stork   *Leptoptilos crumeniferus*   **150-155 cm**

ROY JOHANNESSON

 This huge bird is virtually confined to game reserves, where it is seen either soaring over the bush or scavenging at a kill with vultures. The *enormous bill, unfeathered head and neck, and naked, pink fleshy pouch* render this bird unmistakable. Its wingspan approaches that of the Wandering Albatross, the world's longest at almost 2 m. When threatened or displaying, it clappers its large bill.

17

African Sacred Ibis   *Threskiornis aethiopicus*   **64-82 cm**

L VON HORSTEN

A predominantly *white bird with a black head and neck* which a close range can be seen to be unfeathered. In flight a *narrow blac border to the trailing edge of the wings is visible.* During the breed ing season shows a stripe of bare scarlet skin on leading edge o underwing. Imm. resembles ad. but head and neck feathered white. Occur singly or in small flocks near marshy areas and along the western Cape coas■

Hadeda Ibis   *Bostrychia hagedash*   **76-89 cm**

A WILSON

A dull, *greyish-brown bird with long legs and a long, decurve bill.* At close range an iridescent *bronze patch is conspicuous o the shoulder* and the faint dark and pale lines that run under th eye can be seen. The bill is dark brown but has an almo translucent red ridge. In flight it gives its *distinctive 'ha-ha, ha-ha, de-da' ca* from which it derives its name. It is mainly a woodland ibis but forages i glades and grasslands.

18

African Spoonbill   *Platalea alba*   **90 cm**

G. CUBITT

From a distance, it looks like a white, egret-type bird but when seen at close range, the *long, flattened, spoon-shaped grey and red bill* is diagnostic. The legs, feet and face are bright red. Unlike egrets and herons, it flies with the neck outstretched, and the silhouette of the spoon-shaped bill can be seen. Imm. is duller and has dark-tipped flight feathers. When feeding, scythes its spatulate bill from side to side through water. Occurs on freshwater lakes and estuaries.

Spur-winged Goose   *Plectropterus gambensis*   **75-100 cm**

W.R. TARBOTON

Readily distinguished by its *large size, black and white pied plumage, and pinkish legs and bill*. The male has a fleshy pink knob on the forehead. Female and imm. are dull brown and have less white in the plumage. Out of the breeding season the birds gather in large flocks on open stretches of water and moult their flight feathers, which renders them flightless for several weeks. Gives a most ungoose-like whistle in flight. Found in freshwater habitats surrounded by grassland and agricultural lands.

19

Greater Flamingo   *Phoenicopterus ruber*   **127-140 cm**

J.J BROOKS

Adult

D. BUTCHART

Immature

Larger and paler than the Lesser Flamingo: when seen feeding together, this species almost dwarfs the Lesser Flamingo. As a general rule, the Greater is much whiter, having the pink confined to the wings. The *pink bill with a black tip* is diagnostic. Imm. differs from imm. Lesser Flamingo by being much larger and having a more massive bill. The call is a goose-like honking. Frequents shallow freshwater lakes, salt pans and estuaries.

Lesser Flamingo   *Phoenicopterus minor*   **81-90 cm**

J.J BROOKS

Adult

A WEAVING

Immature

Much smaller than Greater Flamingo and almost always much redder than that species. Imm. and some pale adults have pale plumage but their smaller size and the diagnostic *deep red bill, which at a distance looks black* should rule out confusion. The Lesser and Greater flamingos feed in the same manner: with the head submerged upside down as they filter food through the trough-like bill. Both species flock, sometimes gathering in their thousands. The Lesser Flamingo occurs at shallow freshwater lakes, salt pans and estuaries.

Egyptian Goose *Alopochen aegyptiaca* **63-73 cm**

A. WEAVING

The *chestnut eye patch, white forewings and dark patch on the breast* are diagnostic. When not breeding, occurs in fairly large flocks in open fields, on dams, or on sand bars in rivers. In flocks they tend to be noisy and aggressive, attacking each other and giving loud honking and hissing noises. In flight they form tight flocks in a 'V' formation. Found in freshwater habitats, coastal estuaries and open fields.

White-faced Duck *Dendrocygna viduata* **43-48 cm**

W. R. TARBOTON

The *white face (sometimes stained), chestnut breast and barred flanks* help identify this duck. The stance is also characteristic: the body is held very upright and the neck is stretched to its full length. The call is a three-part whistle 'wee-wee-weeoo' and is often heard at night when flocks move from one feeding ground to another. Found in coastal lagoons and at shallow edges of lakes, but spends much time ashore.

21

Yellow-billed Duck   *Anas undulata*   51-58 cm

N. BRICKELL

The rich, almost *chrome-yellow bill*, which has a black, wedge-shaped patch on top, is diagnostic of this *mottled brown* duck. When the wings are unfolded in flight they show at the base a brilliant blue and green patch (the speculum) which is bordered with black and white. The female gives the characteristic 'quack quack' call whereas the male has a raspy, hissing call. Found on open stretches of freshwater.

Cape Teal   *Anas capensis*   44-48 cm

N. BRICKELL

Smaller than Yellow-billed Duck and easily identified by its *mottled greyish plumage and slightly upturned pink bill*. In flight the wing pattern shows two broad white stripes bordering a small green speculum. Differs from Red-billed Teal by lacking the dark cap of that species. The call is a high-pitched nasal whistle which is mostly given in flight. More common in the drier areas of the region, particularly on saline lagoons and lakes.

Red-billed Teal   *Anas erythrorhyncha*   **43-48 cm**

N BRICKELL

This medium-sized brown and buff mottled duck is easily recognized by its *creamy cheeks which contrast with a dark cap and reddish bill*. In flight it shows a buff speculum. The female's call is a soft 'quack'. Out of the breeding season, this duck gathers in substantial flocks, sometimes with other species, on large stretches of open fresh water.

Cape Shoveler   *Anas smithii*   **53 cm**

N BRICKELL

Distinguished from Yellow-billed Duck by its *black bill* which is spatulate and appears longer than the head. Other features which identify it are the *bright orange legs* and the *powder blue forewings* which are very conspicuous in flight. The female is duller than the male, has a darker head and a smaller patch of blue on the forewings. Occurs in small groups on fresh water, often in company with Yellow-billed Ducks.

23

Southern Pochard *Netta erythrophthalma* **48-51 cm**

Male

 This bird sits low in the water and, on take-off, runs across the water before gaining flight. Rather than upend for its food, this bird habitually dives. The male is distinguished by its *dark plumage, the blue bill and bright red eye*. The female is brown with a pale patch at the base of the bill and a *pale crescentic mark on the sides of the face*. In flight both sexes show a

Female

pale belly and have a broad white strip running down the centre of the wing. Occurs on lakes, dams and vleis; prefers deeper water.

Secretarybird *Sagittarius serpentarius* **140 cm**

 Might be mistaken for a stork or crane when seen striding through the veld but the *short, hooked bill, the black, partly feathered legs and the black, wispy nape plumes* should rule out confusion. In flight it is almost vulture-like except that the *central tail feathers are elongated and project well beyond the end of the tail, as do the long legs*. Most frequently seen in pairs, hunting over open veld, stopping frequently to pick something from the ground or to stamp on some living creature.

White-backed Vulture *Gyps africanus* **95 cm**

J.J. BROOKS

 The common vulture of bushveld game reserves. If seen when the bird is banking in flight or holding its wings outstretched, the *white lower back contrasts with the darker wings* (diagnostic). Imm. is very much darker than ad. and shows less contrast between flight feathers and wing linings. Most often seen in flight, either riding the thermals or high in the air searching the ground for kills. In the early mornings or during cold or overcast, rainy weather, groups can be seen loafing in tree tops. Occurs in open savanna parkland and bushveld.

Yellow-billed Kite *Milvus parasitus* **51-60 cm**

A. WILSON

 The kite seen patrolling roads and frequenting towns and cities. In ad. plumage the *yellow bill and cere* are diagnostic. This large bird of prey is readily distinguished from others by its *forked tail* which it twists in flight from the horizontal to the almost vertical as it steers and manoeuvres through the air. Imm. is darker and has a black, not yellow bill. Call is a whinnying 'kleeeuw' trill. This is the kite commonly seen around human habitation.

Black-shouldered Kite *Elanus caeruleus* **33 cm**

A small, conspicuous bird of prey which is commonly seen sitting on telephone wires and poles, or hovering over the veld or road verges. The ad. is *grey and white with a diagnostic black shoulder patch* and deep, *cherry-red eye*. When perched it occasionally flicks its short white tail. When stooping for food, its wings are held over its back like a parachute. The imm. is dowdier than the ad. and has a buff and brown barred back. It frequents a wide range of habitats from mountains to the coast, and over bushveld and agricultural lands.

H. VON HÖRSTEN

Black-chested Snake-Eagle *Circaetus pectoralis* **63-68 cm**

A. WILSON

In flight this medium-sized raptor can be easily identified as its *white body and underwings, with primaries and secondaries barred black, contrast sharply with the dark brown head and upper breast*. When perched the dark breast, the proportionately very large, rounded dark head with golden-yellow eyes, and the unfeathered yellow legs are evident. Imm. is a rufous version of the ad. Flight action is light and soaring with the bird frequently hovering. Occurs in thornveld, avoiding open grasslands and forests.

ROY JOHANNESSON

Male

L. HES

Immature

Female in flight

An easily identified eagle because of its unusual shape in flight: it appears to have *virtually no tail* and has *very contrasting black and white under-wings*. The wing shape is also unusual, being narrow at the body and tips and broadening towards the centre. The male has a much broader black trailing edge to the wing than the female. Imm. is a brown version of ad. Flight is direct on slightly canted wings and bird careens from side to side. Found over open thornveld in the major game reserves.

D. BUTCHART

Female

African Fish-Eagle *Haliaeetus vocifer* **63-73 cm**

Easily identified by the combination of white head and breast, dark body, chestnut forewings and white tail. Imm. is difficult to distinguish from other brown eagles but it shows a relatively short tail and a shadow image of the adult's white breast. The cry of this bird, a series of gull-like yelps, is very well known in Africa. Always associated with water: coastal lagoons, estuaries, rivers and lakes, but never with the open sea.

N. MYBURGH

P. PICKFORD

Long-crested Eagle *Lophaetus occipitalis* **52-58 cm**

P. PICKFORD

This small, dark brown eagle is instantly recognizable by its *long, wispy crest* and *white-feathered legs*. In flight it shows distinct white 'windows' in the wings and its barred black and white tail. When not soaring, the flight action is swift and direct with shallow wing beats. In natural forests and exotic plantations these birds may be seen perched on dead trees or telephone poles. The call is a loud, piercing 'wee-aah-wee-aah'.

Steppe Buzzard   *Buteo vulpinus* **45-50 cm**

W.R. TARBOTON

Not readily distinguishable from the many similar raptors in the region but most individuals show a pale, broad crescent across the breast. Colours range from almost pale buff to dark brown or black, but the breast pattern is fairly constant. Present only during the summer and then very common, being the most abundant medium-sized raptor seen perched on telephone poles. Flight is strong and direct except when soaring or gliding. Found in open country; avoids deserts and well-wooded regions.

Jackal Buzzard   *Buteo rufofuscus* **55-60 cm**

B. RYAN

Larger than the Steppe Buzzard and not as variable in plumage coloration. When perched appears very dark above, with a bright chestnut breast and barred black and white belly. In flight, the combination of contrasting black and white under-wings and bright chestnut breast and tail is diagnostic. Imm. has rufous brown underparts and a comparatively pale tail. Frequents mountainous areas, where it regularly 'hangs' in the strong winds and updrafts.

29

African Goshawk *Accipiter tachiro* 36-46 cm

P. PICKFORD

N. MYBURGH

Above: adult
Right: immature

A combination of *blue-grey head and dark back* with *pale under parts finely barred with reddish*, helps distinguish ad. Male smaller than female and brighter. Imm. has reddish barring o underparts replaced with large, drop-shaped dark brown spo and shows a dark line down the white throat. Seen most often during ear morning display when it *flies high* over its territory, giving a *short 'whit' c every few seconds*. Occurs in thick evergreen forest, riverine forests in dr areas and exotic plantations.

Gabar Goshawk *Melierax gabar* 28-36 cm

G. CUBITT

P.R.B. STEYN

Adult   **Immature**

Superficially resembles the African Goshawk but has a gre *throat and breast, red, not yellow eyes, cere and legs and a white not dark rump*. Imm. differs markedly, having a rufous-streake and mottled head and breast, but it still shows a white rum A very bold and conspicuous goshawk which regularly sits on expose perches. An uncommon black form occurs which can be identified by its re cere and legs. Occurs in thornveld and open broadleafed woodland.

Southern Pale Chanting Goshawk *Melierax canorus* 48-63 cm

Much larger than either the African or Gabar goshawks and has proportionately *longer legs*. Habitually rests on exposed perches from which it hunts. When put to flight, its *upperparts show a white rump and white trailing edges to the wings and secondaries* which contrast with the darker primaries. Imm. is dark brown above and streaked and blotched with brown below. Name derives from the chanting call given during the breeding season, a piping 'kleeu-kleeu-klu-klu-klu'. Found in the drier western regions and in semi-desert.

Lanner Falcon *Falco biarmicus* 38-45 cm

Above: adult
Below: immature

A medium-sized falcon, the ad. of which shows a *rufous crown and an unmarked pinkish breast*. The imm. has a *buffy streaked crown and heavily streaked underparts*. In flight, this species shows wings which are relatively broad at the base, and which narrow into points. The flight is slow and floppy compared to that of smaller falcons; however, it is rapid when chasing prey and they sometimes execute fast-angled

stoops to strike prey in mid-air. Occurs in a wide range of habitats, from mountains and deserts to open grasslands.

Amur Falcon *Falco amurensis* 30 cm

Male

Female

A small falcon whose overall *dark grey plumage* is relieved on by *contrasting white wing linings and a chestnut vent*. The cere legs and feet are bright red, a feature which can be seen at clos range. The female has a pale greyish head with black mou tachial stripes, grey upperparts, pale underparts heavily streaked wit black, a chestnut vent, and red legs and feet. The imm. is similar to th female but has finer streaking below and has orange, not red legs and fee Flocks frequent open grasslands, and congregate in trees to roost.

Rock Kestrel *Falco rupicolis* 30-33 cm

Male

Very similar to Lesser Kestrel but male has a spotted, not uniform chestnut back, and *lacks blue on his secondaries*. Female very difficult to distinguis from female Lesser Kestrel but Lesser has tendency to form flock which this species does not do. Imm. lacks blue-grey on the head and tail. When hunting it hovers into the wind, remaining station- ary with only its wings moving an tail spread before dropping swiftl onto its prey. Rarely seen away from mountainous terrain.

Female

Immature

Lesser Kestrel   *Falco naumanni*   29-33 cm

Male

Female

Slightly smaller than Rock Kestrel. Male distinguished from the Rock Kestrel by having a *uniform chestnut back, and a blue band across the secondaries* of the upperwing. The white toenails are diagnostic but these are apparent only at close range. Female and imm. closely resemble the female and imm. Rock Kestrel but, in summer, the Lesser Kestrel tends to form large flocks to feed and roost. Flocks often perch on telephone wires from where they swoop over grasslands to catch insects.

Crested Francolin   *Peliperdix sephaena*   33-35 cm

A small, rotund gamebird with a *dark cap that contrasts with a broad white eyebrow stripe*. The upperparts are reddish-brown streaked with buff, and the underparts show a dark freckled neck, throat and breast. Imm. is similar to ad. but has a buff eyebrow stripe. The *tail is often held cocked*, bantam-like, at an angle of 45°. Call is a clear, ringing 'chee-chakla, chee-chakla', given near roosts. Found among heavy tangled growth and along dry river courses in thornveld.

Cape Francolin *Pternistes capensis* 42 cm

J.J. BROOKS

This large gamebird is the francolin most frequently seen in fynbos in the southern Cape. At a distance it appears a *uniform greyish-brown with a dark cap* but at close range it can be seen that the plumage is finely vermiculated with grey and buff. Sexes are similar and the imm. is browner than the ad. Occurs in pairs or small groups and is reluctant to take flight, preferring to run off and hide in undergrowth. Call is a loud, rattling 'cacalak-cacalak'. Occurs in fynbos and wheatfields.

Swainson's Spurfowl *Pternistes swainsonii* 38 cm

P. PICKFORD

This large brown francolin is easily distinguished by having *bare red skin around the eyes and on the throat* and this, combined with its *dark brown legs* is diagnostic. Sexes are similar and the imm. is a dowdier version of the ad. At dusk and dawn the male gives a 'krraae-krraae-krraae' crow from an elevated perch. Occurs in small groups and frequents a variety of habitats, mainly dry thornveld and agricultural lands.

Helmeted Guineafowl   *Numida meleagris*   **58-64 cm**

G. CUBITT

A familiar bird, easily distinguishable by its rotund body and greyish plumage finely spotted with white. The naked blue and red head has red crown casque and wattles. Large groups sometimes form and the birds run around excitedly, chasing one another. When put to flight, they burst from cover and fly clumsily in follow-my-leader style before alighting some distance off. Occurs in grasslands, broadleafed woodland, and thornveld; has become domesticated on farms.

Grey Crowned Crane   *Balearica regulorum*   **105-112 cm**

W. R. TARBOTON

Adult

This large, long-legged bird is unmistakable. When in flight, the *large white wing patches are conspicuous*. Imm. lacks the bold white face patches of the ad. and has a less well-developed bristly golden crown. Has a diagnostic *honking call in flight*. Birds form large flocks when not breeding. Displaying birds dance around facing each other, holding their wings outstretched. Frequents marshes, dams and adjoining grasslands.

35

Blue Crane *Anthropoides paradiseus* **100 cm**

The national bird of South Africa. Overall impression is of a *large, long-legged, greyish bird with a paler head and long drooping tail*. However, the actual tail is very short and the drooping feathers are elongations of inner wing feathers. Feathers on the breast are also elongated and sometimes give the bird a shaggy-breasted appearance. This bird performs a dancing display with the wings outstretched. Associated with freshwater areas and open grasslands but has adapted to agricultural lands.

RAYMONDE JOHANNESSON

Black Crake *Amaurornis flavirostris* **18-20 cm**

H. VON HÖRSTEN

A small, furtive bird with matt black coloration, a *yellow bill and red eyes and legs*. Imm. is a greyish-brown version of the ad. and has a dark bill and dull red legs. A noisy bird, more often heard than seen. More inclined to venture from cover into the open at dawn and dusk, when it may be seen darting over floating vegetation. Will also climb reed stems and can be seen clambering up and clinging to reed stalks. Occurs in marshes and swamps with a thick cover of reeds.

African Purple Swamphen *Porphyrio madagascariensis* **38-46 cm**

 This large, reed-dwelling bird has a bright purplish-blue head and underparts, and a green back offset by bright white under-tail coverts. The *large bill and frontal shield are bright red*, as are the legs and long toes. When creeping about in reedbeds it flicks its tail up and down, revealing the white undertail coverts. It regularly ventures into open areas adjoining thick cover. In flight the legs and toes project well beyond the tail, giving a heron-like outline. Frequents flooded grasslands and thick reedbeds.

Common Moorhen *Gallinula chloropus* **30-36 cm**

 Much smaller than the African Purple Swamphen, which it resembles in that it has a red frontal shield, but this species has *a yellow tip to the bill* and has green, not red legs and toes. Plumage is sooty black but there is a diagnostic *white stripe on flanks*, and the outer undertail coverts are white. Swims with jerky movements and constant flicking of tail, on open water. Imm. is greyish-brown version of ad. Occurs in freshwater areas surrounded by a thick cover of reeds and grass.

Red-knobbed Coot *Fulica cristata* 41-46 cm

ROY JOHANNESSON

Above: adult
Below: immature

W.G. McILLERON

A medium-sized, matt *black, duck-like bird with an ivory-white bill and unfeathered forehead.* The two red knobs situated on the top of the white shield are more conspicuous during the breeding season but are only noticeable at close range. Imm. Is similar to imm. Moorhen but is larger and more grey in appearance, and lacks the white undertail coverts. Sometimes found in large flocks; dives regularly to feed. Likely to occur on any stretch of fresh water, except fast-flowing rivers.

Kori Bustard *Ardeotis kori* 105-135 cm

H. VON HÖRSTEN

This is the heaviest flying bird in the world and is by far the *largest bustard of the region:* its size alone should rule out confusion. The female is noticeably smaller when compared to the male. It is usually seen striding across the open veld, swinging its head and neck with a peculiar backwards and forwards movement. Reluctant to fly unless directly threatened. When displaying, the male gives a deep-throated booming and fluffs out the large white feathered areas on his neck. Found in dry thornveld, open grasslands and semi-desert.

Northern Black Korhaan *Eupodotis afraoides* **52 cm**

Male

Female

This small korhaan is unmistakable, especially when the male is seen in flight display during the breeding season. The male, a striking black, white and barred brown bird, flies into the air and courses over its territory, calling continually. At the end of the display it slowly descends to the ground with slow-motion wing beats and its bright yellow legs dangling. The female is drabber and has the black restricted to the lower belly. Inhabits dry coastal scrub, open grassland and thinly wooded thornveld.

African Jacana *Actophilornis africanus* **28-31 cm**

Adult

Immature

A rufous bird with a darker belly, white throat and breast and yellow foreneck. The *black and white head pattern which offsets a blue frontal shield and bill* is diagnostic. The *toes and toenails, which are exceptionally elongated* to allow walking on floating vegetation, are conspicuous. Imm. is duller, with a paler head and underparts. On landing, this species often holds its wings open over its back. Occurs in flooded grasslands and freshwater areas that have floating vegetation.

39

African Black Oystercatcher   *Haematopus moquini*   **44 cm**

A WEAVING

A medium-sized *black wader which has an obvious orange-red bill*, dull pink legs and a bright orange ring around the eye. Imm. is dowdier and has a less vividly coloured bill. When in flight, the bird appears all black and has no wing markings although a few individuals may show some white on the underparts. Usually found in pairs but larger groups form between breeding seasons. Found along rocky coasts and on sandy beaches.

White-fronted Plover   *Charadrius marginatus*   **16 cm**

A WEAVING

A small, pale plover likely to be confused with imm. Kittlitz's Plover but this species generally has a paler breast, a much *paler, sandier coloured back and a black marking on the fore head*. Imm. lacks dark marking on head and is paler than ad. with buff edging to feathers of the back and mantle. Frequents sandy beaches, muddy coastal areas and large river systems.

Kittlitz's Plover   *Charadrius pecuarius*   **14-15 cm**

Above: adult
Below: immature

This small plover is distinguished by its cinnamon-coloured underparts and by the *black line on the forehead which extends behind the eye on to the nape*. Imm. lacks the black head markings of ad. but is darker than similar White-fronted Plover and has a dark shoulder mark. Not often seen on open beaches, it occurs in small flocks sometimes far from water; prefers short grassy areas and dried muddy patches.

Three-banded Plover   *Charadrius tricollaris*   **18 cm**

This small plover has an overall elongated appearance and frequently bobs its head and tail. The *double black breast band* is diagnostic; this species also shows a *grey face and throat*, red eye ring and red base to the bill. Although it occurs singly or in pairs on smaller stretches of water, at certain times of the year large numbers may gather at favoured freshwater dams.

Grey Plover *Pluvialis squatarola* **28-31 cm**

A WILSON

A medium-sized wading bird which is drab grey, lightly speckled with white above, and off-white to white below. The head is relatively large and the bill is short and black. Only in flight are the diagnostic *black armpits* clearly visible. In breeding plumage (rarely seen in the region) the underparts are jet black and the upperparts are spangled with silver. When feeding, these birds remain motionless and then dart forward to pick up their prey. Found on open estuaries, bays and lagoons.

Crowned Lapwing *Vanellus coronatus* **30-31 cm**

W.R. TARBOTON

A very familiar wader not associated with water but commonly encountered in towns and villages where it frequents grassy road verges and open sportsfields. Readily identified by its brownish plumage with a white belly and the diagnostic *black cap surrounded by a white 'halo'*. The bird's legs are bright vermilion, as is the bill base. Very active and noisy at night when the raucous 'kreeep' call can be heard.

Blacksmith Lapwing   *Vanellus armatus* **31 cm**

H. VON HORSTEN

This large *black, white and grey bird* is the easiest lapwing (plover) to identify and the bold wing pattern makes it readily distinguishable in flight. The imm. is a duller version of ad. with brown feathering replacing the black. When alarmed and put to flight, the bird gives a rapid, *metallic 'tink tink'* call and, if the breeding territory is invaded, it will dive-bomb the intruder. Found near damp areas and wetland edges and adjoining grasslands.

Ruddy Turnstone   *Arenaria interpres* **21-24 cm**

A. WILSON

This small wader can be seen running over pebbly beaches or poking about in strands of rotting seaweed. Its *bill is short, slightly flattened and upturned* and with this it busily *overturns small stones* or prods aside seaweed in search of food. The upperparts are dark and the pale underparts show irregular dark markings at the front and sides of the breast. The legs are relatively short and are *bright orange with darker joints*. In flight it shows *heavily patterned wings and tail*.

43

Common Sandpiper *Actitis hypoleucos* **19-21 cm**

A WILSON

This small, usually solitary wader has a peculiar habit of *bobbing backward and forward* between short bursts of running. *is uniformly drab brown above and white below, with the whi on the breast curving up and over the shoulder*. In flight the wing are held slightly *bowed downwards and are flicked rapidly between sho glides*. Flight call is a characteristic 'tee tee tee'. It occurs in a wide range wetland habitats.

Wood Sandpiper *Tringa glareola* **19-21 cm**

A WILSON

Has a bobbing action similar to that of Common Sandpiper b not as exaggerated. Identification points are the *brownish bac well spotted with buff or white, the white rump and barred ta* (best seen in flight), a pale grey underwing, and long greenis yellow legs which project well beyond the tail in flight. When alarmed ar in flight gives a shrill 'chif if if' call. Spotting on upperparts appears muc reduced when plumage is worn. Occurs on dams, vleis, bays and estuarie

Curlew Sandpiper *Calidris ferruginea* **18-23 cm**

L. HES

A small wading bird with longish legs and a long decurved bill. Appears very grey in the field; in flight shows a broad white rump and a noticeable wing bar. Breeding plumage is totally different: rufous underparts and brightly patterned upperparts, but the whitish rump is still evident. Feeds by walking belly-deep in water and probing its bill into mud. Found in a wide variety of wetland habitats, but is most common in coastal estuaries.

Common Greenshank *Tringa nebularia* **30-35 cm**

J.C. SINCLAIR

A medium-sized, very grey wader which has a *slightly upturned, dark-tipped grey bill* and long, *greyish-olive legs*. In flight it shows a *conspicuous white rump which extends up the back in a white wedge*. It is often seen running around in the shallows chasing small fish. It gives a ringing 'chew-chew-chew' in flight and when startled. Frequents a wide range of fresh- and saltwater wetlands.

45

Bar-tailed Godwit *Limosa lapponica* **38 cm**

L. HES

This large wader is easily recognized by its *very long, upturned bill, the basal half of which is pink*. The non-breeding bird is mottled grey and brown above and white below, but in breeding plumage the underparts assume a rich orange-brown colour. In flight it shows a *white rump and finely barred tail, and dark upperwings.* Frequents estuaries, bays and muddy-edged lakes where it freely wades out into deep water to feed. Sometimes gathers in large groups to roost.

Common Whimbrel *Numenius phaeopus* **40-43 cm**

A. WILSON

From a distance, might be confused with the Bar-tailed Godwit, but this bird has a long decurved bill. At closer range, the diagnostic *black stripes on the head*, bisected by a pale stripe down the centre of the crown, and the pale eye-stripe can be seen. In flight it shows a *conspicuous white rump which extends on to the lower back.* Invariably gives a staccato whistled call note when flushed. Found in estuaries, coastal lagoons and bays.

Pied Avocet   *Recurvirostra avosetta*   **43 cm**

W.R. TARBOTON

 An unmistakable, large black and white wader with a *long, very thin upturned bill*. The legs are long and blue and the feet are partly webbed. In flight the *three black patches in each wing* make a very striking pattern. Frequents lakes and vleis where the birds regularly swim, dipping their heads and bills under water. Gives a sharp, rattling call in flight. Occurs in pairs when breeding but forms large flocks at other times.

Black-winged Stilt   *Himantopus himantopus*   **38 cm**

W.R. TARBOTON

 This wader is distinguished by the combination of its exceptionally *long pink legs* and its *black and white plumage*. The bill is long, black, very thin and pointed. Female and imm. have the black on the back and wings tinged with brown; the imm. has extensive brown markings on its hindneck and head. The breeding male shows a black nape and crown. Rarely flocks. Inhabits marshes, vleis, saltpans and flooded areas.

Spotted Thick-knee   *Burhinus capensis*   **43 cm**

J J BROOKS

A *cryptically coloured* wading bird with a large head and big yellow eyes. The bill is short and yellow at its base and the legs are greenish-yellow. Plumage is mottled brown, buff and black and in flight shows two small *white patches in the upperwing*. Occurs away from water and is active at night, resting up during the day under bushes or in other shade. When defending its territory, the wings are held fully spread and slightly forward to display the white wing patches. Found in dry sparse bush and overgrazed areas.

Subantarctic Skua   *Catharacta antarctica*   **60-66 cm**

J C SINCLAIR

A *large brown seabird* which resembles an imm. Cape Gull but lacks the white rump and shows conspicuous *white patches at the base of the primaries*. This bird, the largest member of the skua family, has a heavy body, broad-based wings and mottled brown plumage. Some birds show a tawny head and throat. Flight is normally slow and ponderous but when chasing another seabird to pirate its prey, it thrusts forward on powerful wings. Found over open oceans, rarely venturing inshore.

48

Cape Gull   *Larus vetula*   **55-65 cm**

Above: adult
Below: immature

The largest gull in the region. The ad. is easily identified by its white body, jet black back and upperwings and bright yellow bill with an orange spot at the tip. Imm. plumage is very variable but in the first year the bird is very dark brown with a pale rump; it becomes paler with age. Found at estuaries, and at coastal and inshore waters.

Grey-headed Gull   *Larus cirrocephalus*   **40-42 cm**

Above: adult
Below: immature

Differs from Hartlaub's Gull by having a dove-grey head, pale eye and bright red bill, legs and feet. It is also slightly larger bodied and has a longer, heavier bill than Hartlaub's. Imm. Grey-headed has more extensive dark markings on the head, paler legs, a pink bill with a dark tip and a more extensive black tip to the tail than imm. Hartlaub's. Although this gull occurs in coastal and freshwater areas, it breeds inland, away from the sea.

Hartlaub's Gull   *Larus hartlaubii*   **36-38 cm**

L· HES

Slightly smaller than Grey-headed Gull with a *darker red bill and legs*, and dark eyes. In breeding plumage shows a *faint grey hood*, but in non-breeding plumage has a completely white head. Imm. has faint brownish markings on the head, the black tip to the tail is either reduced or absent, and it has a brown, not two-tone bill as in imm. Grey-headed Gull. This is the small gull common along the southern Cape coast.

Caspian Tern   *Sterna caspia*   **47-54 cm**

A. WEAVING

Non-breeding

The *largest tern* in the world, it is instantly recognizable by its conspicuous *coral-red bill*. In breeding plumage has totally black cap but when not breeding and in imm. plumage has the cap streaked black and white. Imm. has an orange bill and dark-edged back feathers. In flight the shallowly forked tail and the black tips to the underside of the primaries can be

Breeding

seen. Call is loud, harsh 'kraaak'; imm. gives a weak, nasal whistle. Found in the vicinity of large rivers, estuaries, bays, lagoons and inshore waters.

Swift Tern *Sterna bergii* **46-49 cm**

Smaller than the Caspian Tern, this species has a *yellow not red bill*. At long range it shows a plain white underwing. In breeding plumage has black cap ending just before the bill, imparting a white forehead; when not breeding has variable amount of black on forehead but appears mostly white or grizzled. Imm. has *mottled upperparts and extensive black on head* but still shows yellow bill. Frequents islands, larger estuaries and bays.

N. MYBURGH

Right: breeding
Below: non-breeding

P. PICKFORD

Common Tern *Sterna hirundo* **31-35 cm**

CAPE BIRD CLUB

During summer, the most abundant small tern on the southern African coast. Has many features in common with most small, non-breeding terns (grey upperparts, white underparts, and a partially developed black cap). Subtle aids to identification are the long, slightly decurved bill and uniform grey rump. In breeding plumage (attained in March-April), the bird has a wholly black cap, pale grey underparts, a very long forked tail and a bright red, black-tipped bill. Often forms vast roosting flocks on beaches and at river mouths.

White-winged Tern *Chlidonias leucopterus* **20-23 cm**

The most abundant small freshwater tern in our area. The non-breeding plumage is *pale grey and white* with *small amounts of black on the head and underwing*. In breeding plumage (seldom seen in the region) the bird is a striking contrast of *black, grey and white*, with the *silvery forewings* being most noticeable. Flight can be almost butterfly-like and is very buoyant as the bird dips over water to pick up food. Occurs mostly over freshwater areas but is also found at larger estuaries.

Below: breeding

Above: non-breeding

A. WILSON

Namaqua Sandgrouse *Pterocles namaqua* **25 cm**

A pigeon-sized bird and, in the region, the only sandgrouse with a *long pointed tail*. In flight has very rapid wing beats and often gives its nasal 'kalke-vein' call which reveals its presence. The male has a buff-spotted back and a white and chestnut breast band; the female is cryptically mottled and streaked with buff and brown but still shows the pointed tail. Inhabits dry grasslands, and true and semi-deserts.

Above: female
Below: male

N. MYBURGH

Rock Dove   *Columba livia*   **33 cm**

This is the *common street pigeon* familiar to anyone who lives in a city. It occurs in a variety of plumages: the most common colour combination is a dark grey body, an iridescent sheen on the neck, a white rump and pale grey wings which show two black bars. Away from cities, it is often seen in the vicinity of farmsteads or in flocks of racing pigeons winging across the veld.

Speckled Pigeon   *Columba guinea*   **30-34 cm**

Appears very dark in the field but, at close range, the finely *white-speckled reddish back* and wings and the *bare red skin around the eyes* are diagnostic. Occurs in flocks, and is sometimes found in substantial numbers over stubble cornfields; has adapted to urban life and is frequently seen on ledges of buildings. Call is very owl-like, with a deep resonant 'hoo-hoo' and it echoes through the cliff caves and ledges this species frequents in nature.

African Olive-Pigeon   *Columba arquatrix*   **37-42 cm**

By far the *largest dove or pigeon* in the region and appears the darkest of all. Only in bright sunlight or at close range can the *bright yellow bill, bare skin around the eyes and on the legs and feet be seen*. The plumage is a mixture of dark maroons, grey and blue, finely speckled with white. In flight the bird appears almost black but the sun often highlights the yellow bill or feet. Found in evergreen forests and exotic plantations.

Red-eyed Dove   *Streptopelia semitorquata*   **30-33 cm**

The largest and darkest of the 'ring-neck' doves. The eye and the bare skin surrounding it are red – a feature normally seen only at close range. Unlike the Cape Turtle-Dove it shows *no white in the tail* but it does have a *grey band on the undertail* and a diagnostic *black band at the base of the tail*. Imm. is very similar to ad. but has a reduced ring on the neck. Ranges from dry bushveld to coastal forests; has adapted to towns and cities.

Cape Turtle-Dove *Streptopelia capicola* **25-28 cm**

H VON HORSTEN

The 'ring-neck' dove which shows a diagnostic *white tip and sides to the tail in flight*. This dove is much paler and *smaller than the Red-eyed Dove* which lacks white in the tail. Probably the most abundant dove in the region, its three-note call is a familiar background sound in the veld. Display flight consists of the bird flying up at low angle and then descending slowly with wings and tail spread. It occurs in a wide range of habitats; avoids coastal forest.

Laughing Dove *Streptopelia senegalensis* **22-24 cm**

N. MYBURGH

Smaller than the Cape Turtle-Dove and *lacks the black hind collar* of that species. It has a *pinkish-grey body, pale blue forewings and a finely black-speckled breast*. In flight lacks the white tail tip seen in the Cape Turtle-Dove but has conspicuous white outertail feathers. The call, from which it derives its name, is a chortled cooing. Not present in arid areas but inhabits a wide range of bush and farmlands and occurs in many towns and cities.

55

Namaqua Dove   *Oena capensis*   **28 cm**

N. MYBURGH

Male

A small-bodied dove which has a *long pointed tail, and a black face and throat*. In flight the combination of the long pointed tail, pale underparts and chestnut flight feathers render this bird unmistakable. Shows iridescent blue spots on the wings. The imm. and female lack the black face of the male but show a shorter pointed tail and chestnut flight feathers. Prefers drier regions such as thornveld, scrub and semi-desert.

J.J. BROOKS

Female

Emerald-Spotted Wood-Dove   *Turtur chalcospilos*   **16-20 cm**

P. PICKFORD

A small dove which is often seen in game reserves when it is flushed from roadsides or congregates at waterholes. In flight it shows *reddish wing patches* and *two black bars on its rump*; it is only at close range and in sunlight that the *green wing spots* can be seen. The characteristic call is a series of descending 'du-du' notes. Found in thornveld and dry, broadleafed woodland.

Brown-headed Parrot   *Poicephalus cryptoxanthus*   **24-25 cm**

A. WILSON

A small, *brown-headed parrot which at rest appears very green* and is difficult to see in a leafy canopy; often it is the bird's screeches and squawks that indicate its presence. In flight, which is very rapid, the *bright yellow underwings* are visible. Imm. is a duller version of ad. Frequents thornveld, riverine forest and open woodland.

Knysna Turaco   *Tauraco corythaix*   **40-42 cm**

ROY JOHANNESSON

A large *green bird with a long tail and crest*. Distinguished from the Purple-crested Turaco by its greenish plumage, white-tipped crest and whitish marks above and below the eye. Groups frequent tree canopies where they run along the larger branches, raising and lowering their tails. In flight, they show *brilliant red patches on the wing tips*. The call is a loud, far-carrying 'kow kow kow'. Occurs in dense evergreen forests.

Purple-crested Turaco *Musophaga porphyreolopha* 43 cm

A. WILSON

Superficially resembles the Knysna Turaco but is very much *darker*. It has a *dark purple crest which appears black* unless seen in good light, it lacks the white markings and crest tips of the Knysna Turaco and has bare red skin around the eyes. It behaves very much like the Knysna Turaco in that it keeps to tree tops where it leaps nimbly from branch to branch, showing the bright red wing patches. Found in evergreen, coastal and riverine forests.

Grey Go-Away-Bird *Corythaixoides concolor* 48 cm

A large, uniformly *grey bird with a long tail and crest*, it is often seen in groups perched on the top of thorn trees, where it looks like a giant mousebird. Flight is strong, with flapping alternating with gliding. Members of a group fly in single file, in follow-my-leader fashion. The call is a diagnostic 'go-away' or variations of this; when calling, the bird raises its crest and flicks its tail. Frequents thornveld and dry woodland.

ROY JOHANNESSON

ROY JOHANNESSON

White-backed Mousebird   *Colius colius*   **34 cm**

 Most likely to be confused with the Speckled Mousebird from which it is best differentiated at rest by having *red legs and feet and a pale bill tipped with black*. In flight the *back shows a white stripe narrowly bordered with black* and this is diagnostic. It behaves in much the same manner as the Speckled Mousebird but is more agile and has a more powerful flight. Inhabits thornveld, fynbos scrub and arid regions.

Speckled Mousebird   *Colius striatus*   **35 cm**

 A small, drab, *long-tailed bird* which occurs in small groups and creeps about in bushes, mouselike, and hangs from branches. When flushed, the birds fly to the next bush in 'follow-my-leader' fashion and virtually crash-land. Distinguishable from the White-backed and Red-faced mousebirds by its *black face, black and white bill, and brown legs*. Occurs in thick tangled bush, and fruiting trees in suburban gardens.

H. VON HORSTEN

N. MYBURGH

Red-faced Mousebird   *Urocolius indicus*   34 cm

A WEAVING

Easily distinguished from other mousebirds by being pale *greyish in colour* and by having the *bill base and the naked skin around the eye bright red*. Flight action is very different from that of other mousebirds in that it is direct, fast and powerful with the birds flying in small groups or in single file. The call is a diagnostic three- or four-note whistled 'whee-whe-whe'. Found in thornveld, open broadleafed woodland and suburban gardens; avoids dense forest and desert.

Red-chested Cuckoo   *Cuculus solitarius*   28-31 cm

W.G. McILLERON

This cuckoo's *three-note call 'weet-weet-weeeoo'* is diagnostic and is often the only indication of the bird's presence as it is extremely difficult to discern in the leafy canopy it frequents. It is normally only seen as it swiftly departs, when the very *dark back and chestnut breast* instantly identify it. Imm. is very dark above and is heavily barred black below. A bird of evergreen forest and exotic plantations.

Black Cuckoo *Cuculus clamosus* **28-31 cm**

 More often heard than seen but is fairly obvious when glimpsed in the canopy or when foraging lower down in a tree. It might be confused with its host, the Fork-tailed Drongo, but lacks the forked tail. It differs from the black morph Jacobin Cuckoo by *lacking the crest and white wing patches*. The call is a mournful, droning 'whooo-wheeee', repeated frequently. Inhabits woodland and forests, exotic plantations and suburban gardens.

Jacobin Cuckoo *Oxylophus jacobinus* **33-34 cm**

 An all-black morph occurs which might be mistaken for a Black Cuckoo but this species shows a diagnostic wispy crest and white patches at the base of the primaries. Pale phase birds are black and white with a long tail, crested head, white wing patches and lack any striping on the underparts. It is most often detected by its 'klee-kleeu' call. This species occurs in woodlands, preferring thornveld.

61

Diderick Cuckoo *Chrysococcyx caprius* **17-19 cm**

W.G. McILLERON

P.R.B. STEYN

Adult   **Immature**

During summer the 'dee-dee-dee-deederic' call is a familiar soun in and around the weaver and bishop colonies that these bir parasitize. When not calling they can be distinguished from th similar Klaas's Cuckoo by their more contrasting bottle-green an white plumage, more extensive white behind the eye, and white flashes on th wings and shoulders. At close range the bright cherry-coloured eye can b seen. This species occurs in open grasslands with stands of trees, in thornvel and exotic plantations.

Burchell's Coucal *Centropus burchelli* **40-41 cm**

A. WEAVING

Most often seen sitting on an exposed perch either drying itsel after a downpour or sunning itself in the early morning. It is a large bird and is easily identified by its *black cap, chestnut back and wings and long black floppy tail.* Some birds have a white-flecked head with a broad white eyebrow stripe. The call, usually given before or after rain, is a liquid, bubbling series of notes. Normally shy and furtive, this species occurs in long grass, riverine scrub and reedbeds.

Spotted Eagle-Owl   *Bubo africanus*   **43-50 cm**

P PICKFORD

 The most frequently seen *large owl with 'ear' tufts*. It is normally a *greyish-brown mottled and barred* bird but it may be *richer brown in colour*. This owl has adapted to suburbia where it is a regular sight on driveways or roofs and its hooting call may be heard in the evenings. If disturbed at its daytime roost in a thickly foliaged tree, it holds its large yellow eyes partially closed. Frequents a variety of habitats, but avoids dense forest.

Barn Owl   *Tyto alba*   **33-36 cm**

 Active at dusk or dawn, this owl appears very pale and is totally silent on the wing. At rest during the day, the white, heart-shaped face with black eyes, and faintly spotted, light buffy underparts with richer golden upperparts identify this owl. When startled during the day, it moves from side to side while peering at the intruder. Found near human habitation but will roost in caves, mineshafts and hollow trees.

P R B STEYN

African Scops-Owl *Otus senegalensis* 15-17 cm

The call of this *diminutive owl* is an often-heard 'night noise' in the bushveld and it is usually taken to be a frog. When seen in torchlight, the *tiny size, greyish 'bark-like' plumage and long ear tufts* identify this bird. When roosting during the day, it compresses its body, huddles against a tree trunk and slits its eyes, making it almost impossible to detect. Occurs in bushveld and dry open woodland.

Fiery-necked Nightjar *Caprimulgus pectoralis* 22-24 cm

Nightjars are nocturnal and are very difficult to observe; even if flushed during the day, identification depends on a few seconds' view before the bird vanishes. The features to look for in the male are the white markings on the tail and wings, and in the female the *white outertail spots* which differentiate it from similar nightjars. The bird's call, which is given at night, is a diagnostic, whistled 'whuee-whe-whe-whe-whe-whe' with the last notes rapidly descending in pitch. Found at the edge of woodland in bushveld and exotic plantations.

Malachite Kingfisher *Alcedo cristata* **13-14 cm**

L. VON HORSTEN

Usually seen fleetingly as it passes low over the water. When fishing, remains motionless for long periods, perched on a reed stem or branch overhanging water, and is often overlooked. The crown is *barred black and turquoise*, the back is an *iridescent blue* with a turquoise rump, and the *underparts are reddish-brown and white*. The bill in the ad. is bright red and is a useful identification feature, but the imm. has a blackish bill. Frequents reedbeds surrounding lakes, lagoons, streams and rivers.

Woodland Kingfisher *Halcyon senegalensis* **20-22 cm**

W. R. TARBOTON

Much more brightly coloured than the Brown-hooded Kingfisher and has a *black lower mandible and red upper mandible*, not an all-red bill. Differs further from the Brown-hooded Kingfisher by having a *blue head, back and tail*. A common bushveld bird, it is often seen perched on a tree top displaying with outstretched wings and giving its sharp, piercing 'trrp-trrrrrrrr' call. The imm. is dowdier and its black lower mandible shows some red patches. Inhabits thornveld, broadleafed woodland and riverine forest.

Brown-hooded Kingfisher *Halcyon albiventris* 19-20 cm

A much *duller bird than other red-billed kingfishers*. Eas[ily] identified by its *all-red bill, brownish, streaked head,* chestn[ut] patches on the sides of the breast, and streaked flanks. Sho[ws] less blue on wings and lower back than the Woodla[nd] Kingfisher, but this is still very evident in flight. Sits motionless on per[ch] waiting for prey and in a blue flash will descend rapidly to the ground [to] snatch an insect or lizard. Occurs in thornveld, open broadleafed woodla[nd] and coastal forests; has adapted to suburban gardens.

Pied Kingfisher *Ceryle rudis* 23-25 cm

Male

The only kingfisher to have a *pied black and white plumage*. T[he] bill is exceptionally long. The male has a double black bre[ast] band whereas the female has only a single. Before plunging f[or] its fish prey, this species either perches on a branch overhang[ing] water or it hovers and then dives. It sometimes occurs in small grou[ps] whose members interact excitedly, giving a twittering call and a hig[h]-pitched 'chik-chik'. Found on any stretch of open water, coastal lagoons a[nd] rock pools.

66

Striped Kingfisher *Halcyon chelicuti* **16-18 cm**

A WEAVING

A small, dull bushveld kingfisher which is easily recognized by its dark-capped appearance which contrasts with a pale collar, the fine streaking on its breast, and a red and black bill. The call is a high-pitched 'cheer-cherrrrr' and, when calling in display, it will raise its wings to show the black and white patterned underwing and blue back. The latter is more obvious in flight. It frequents thornveld, and riverine and coastal forests.

Narina Trogon *Apaloderma narina* **30-34 cm**

L HES

Male

Frequents the canopy and mid-storey of forests and is never easy to see. Although it is very brightly coloured, the bird habitually sits with its green back to the observer and is thus well camouflaged in its leafy surroundings. A front view will reveal the *bright red breast and belly with a whitish undertail*. The female lacks the green throat of the male, has a duller crimson breast and is generally dowdier. It occurs in riverine and evergreen forests and dense, broadleafed woodland.

67

European Bee-eater *Merops apiaster* 26-28 cm

In flight this bird shows a *dazzling array of colours with its chestnut to golden back contrasting with turquoise-blue underparts* and almost translucent rufous wings. At rest the bright yellow throat bordered by a narrow black gorget can be seen. The imm. has a greenish back and pale blue underparts. Groups fly high, uttering the characteristic, far-carrying peawhistle-like 'prrrup' call. Frequents thornveld, broad-leafed woodland and adjacent grassy areas.

H. VON HÖRSTEN

Little Bee-eater *Merops pusillus* 14-17 cm

N. MYBURGH

The smallest bee-eater and probably the most widespread and common. Easily identified by its *small size, green back and buff underparts, yellow throat with black gorget*, and square or slightly forked tail which lacks projections. Always seen in pairs or small groups hunting insects from low perches. The russet underwings are conspicuous when the bird dashes out to catch insects. Frequents edges of thornveld and clearings in coastal forests.

68

White-fronted Bee-eater   *Merops bullockoides*   **22-24 cm**

In flight appears very *green with a dark blue undertail* but at rest the *red and white throat and white forehead* are diagnostic. Has a square-ended tail and lacks pointed tail projections. Hunts insects from a perch, sallying forth to take prey in flight, and then returns to the same perch. Nest colonies, which are sometimes large, are situated in steep sandy cliffs cut by wide, slow-moving rivers. The birds are active and noisy around the nests, giving nasal 'qrrruk-qrruk' calls.

A. WEAVING

European Roller   *Coracias garrulus*   **30-31 cm**

W R TARBOTON

Superficially resembles the Lilac-breasted Roller but *lacks the long outertail feathers* of that species and has a *clear blue breast* and has much more *chestnut on the back*. In flight it appears paler than the Lilac-breasted Roller and has a *square-ended tail*. Although the imm. Lilac-breasted Roller has a square-ended tail, it has a lilac-washed breast. Catches insects on the wing or by swooping from a perch to the ground. Found in thornveld and open grasslands with scattered trees.

Lilac-breasted Roller   *Coracias caudatus*   32-36 cm

A WEAVING

This species is commonly seen in some game reserves. It frequently perches on telephone poles and wires, from where it swoops to catch its insect prey. In flight it shows a range of pale and dark blues in the wing. At rest, the lilac breast and long pointed outertail feathers are diagnostic. When displaying, the male will perform a complex flight in which he rolls from side to side on the downward stoop. Occurs in mixed areas of thornveld, broadleafed woodland and along roadsides.

African Hoopoe   *Upupa africana*   25-28 cm

A WEAVING

The combination of a *pinkish-brown body* and striking *black and white wings and tail* is diagnostic. The *black- and white-tipped crest* is often held closed but the bird will raise it if alarmed or on alighting. When feeding it walks with a jerky gait and probes its long bill into the ground, searching for insects. The call is a soft 'hoop-hoop-hoop'. Inhabits thornveld, broadleafed woodland, and parks and gardens.

70

The ad. is a large, *glossy blue and green bird with a long, gradu-ated, white-tipped tail* and a *long, red, decurved bill* and red feet. The imm. is not as glossy as the ad. and has a black, not red bill. Small groups clamber through foliage and up tree trunks, using their bills to probe for insects. The cackling call is sometimes given by the whole group; birds sway backwards and forwards while calling. Occurs in woodland and thornveld.

Common Scimitarbill *Rhinopomastus cyanomelas* **28-30 cm**

Likely to be confused only with the imm. Green Wood-Hoopoe which has a black bill but this species is *smaller and its bill is much thinner and more decurved*. In flight the white patches in the wings and the long, graduated, white-tipped tail can be seen. It appears black at a distance but, in direct sunlight, the glossy purple and blue plumage is evident. Frequents thornveld and dry, broadleafed woodland.

71

Trumpeter Hornbill *Bycanistes bucinator* **58-60 cm**

A. WILSON

Male

This large black and white hornbill is instantly recognizable by its *black bill and large casque*, and its *red face*. The female and imm. have smaller casques, pied plumage similar to that of the male, and reddish faces. The species has a dipping flight action with noisy wing flapping interspersed with glides. The call is a diagnostic wailing, resembling the sound of a baby crying. Found in evergreen, coastal and riverine forests.

African Grey Hornbill *Tockus nasutus* **46-51 cm**

W.R. TARBOTON

Male

P. PICKFORD

Female

The *only small hornbill that has a dark bill*. The female might be mistaken for a Southern Yellow-billed Hornbill because the top of her bill is creamy yellow but she has a dark head and breast, and a conspicuous white eyebrow stripe. The imm. is very similar to the female. Flight action is very floppy and buoyant. The call is a series of piping notes. Occurs in thornveld and broadleafed woodland in drier areas.

Red-billed Hornbill *Tockus erythrorhynchus* **40-51 cm**

A. WEAVING

Plumage resembles the Southern Yellow-billed Hornbill's but this species has a *shorter, more slender red bill*. Distinguished from all other hornbills with red bills by its *small size*. Imm. has a duller, less well-developed bill and has buff, not white spotting on the wings. Display consists of the bird bobbing its head and giving 'kokwe-kokwe-kokwe' call with its wings held slightly open. Usually occurs singly or in pairs but may flock when not breeding. Inhabits thornveld and mopane woodland.

Southern Yellow-billed Hornbill *Tockus leucomelas* **55 cm**

A. WEAVING

Resembles the Red-billed Hornbill but is far larger and has a more *massive yellow, not red bill*. The female Grey Hornbill, which has a creamy yellow top to her bill and might be confused with this species, has a dark head and breast. Feeds mostly on the ground where it hops, not walks; frequents picnic sites in game reserves. Display is similar to that of the Red-billed Hornbill: it spreads its wings while giving its 'tok-tok-tork-tork' call notes. Inhabits thornveld and broadleafed woodland.

Southern Ground-Hornbill   *Bucorvus leadbeateri* **90-100 cm**

An unmistakable, *turkey-sized* bird with a *long, decurved black bill* and conspicuous *naked red face and throat*, the latter often slightly inflated with air. Imm. differs from ad. by showing yellow, not red face and throat patches. Occurs in small groups or family parties which *walk, on tiptoes*, through the veld. Usually flies only when deliberately flushed and has a cumbersome flight; shows *broad white wing patches*. Call is a loud booming 'oomph oomph' given early in the morning. Occurs in open grassland in thornveld, broadleafed woodland and upland grasslands.

Above right: adult
Right: immature

Black-collared Barbet   *Lybius torquatus* **18-20 cm**

Instantly recognizable by the *bright red face and throat broad bordered with black*. This bulbul-sized bird has a short ta chunky body and very thick bill. Imm. has the face and thro brown, streaked with red and orange. Pairs duet in display sitting together and bobbing up and down, giving a ringing 'too-puddl call. Occurs in thornveld, broadleafed woodland and coastal forest.

74

Acacia Pied Barbet   *Tricholaema leucomelas*   **16-18 cm**

N. MYBURGH

Similar in shape to the Black-collared Barbet but is smaller and has diagnostic *black and white plumage, a red forehead and yellow spotting on the back* and wings. Might be confused with the Red-fronted Tinkerbird but is much larger, has a black bib and more massive bill. Mostly solitary or in pairs and gives a nasal 'nehh-nehh' or a Hoopoe-like 'doo-doo-doo' call. Found in dry broadleafed woodland, hornveld and arid scrub.

Red-fronted Tinkerbird   *Pogoniulus pusillus*   **9-10,5 cm**

W. G. McILLERON

This small barbet might be confused with the larger Acacia Pied Barbet but has a white throat and much more yellow streaking on the upperparts. Very similar to the Yellow-fronted Tinkerbird but has a *red, not yellow forehead* and generally has brighter yellow streaking above. Usually solitary but may gather in small numbers at fruiting trees. Occurs in moist broadleafed woodland and forest.

75

Yellow-fronted Tinkerbird *Pogoniulus chrysoconus* **11 cm**

B. RYAN

Very similar to the Red-fronted Tinkerbird, but their ranges do not overlap so there is little chance of confusion. The yellow of the forehead is not readily discernible on this tiny barbet and the *overall appearance is that of a greyish streaked bird with a yellow wash on the wings and pale underparts*. When seen, the yellow forehead can sometimes appear a rich orange colour but it never attains the bright red of the Red-fronted Tinkerbird. The call is a continual and monotonous 'konk konk konk' metallic sound and is repeated rapidly.

Crested Barbet *Trachyphonus vaillantii* **23-24 cm**

N. MYBURGH

The largest of the barbets, this species is unmistakable with its orange-yellow face, *black shaggy crest and broad black breast band*, white and golden speckled back, and crimson rump. Much more terrestrial than other barbets, it hops around with an upright stance, but when it does fly, the flight is rapid and direct. The song is a diagnostic trilling which has been likened to the ringing of a muffled alarm clock. Occurs in open broadleafed woodland, thornveld and riverine forest; has adapted to suburban gardens.

Lesser Honeyguide   *Indicator minor* 13-15 cm

W G McILLERON

This small and unobtrusive bird can easily be detected by its distinctive call – a far-carrying 'klew klew klew' – which is given from the same perch and is repeated regularly. It is overall dull greyish, with a greenish wash on the wing coverts, a small dark moustachial stripe and conspicuous white outertail feathers. It is often seen being harassed by barbets and, as it dashes through the canopy, its white tail feathers are conspicuous.

Golden-tailed Woodpecker   *Campethera abingoni* 18-20 cm

The loud, nasal 'wheeeeeeaa' shriek and bill tapping on wood often reveal the presence of this bird. When it is seen clinging to a tree, the best identification features to look for are the *streaked underparts, buff and yellow spots on the olive back, and the black and red crown and red moustachial stripe.* It climbs vertical tree trunks with jerky movements, using its tail as a brace. Found in thornveld, open broadleafed woodland and coastal forests.

W R TARBOTON

right: male

77

Cardinal Woodpecker   *Dendropicos fuscescens*   14-15 cm

 Very much smaller than the Golden-tailed Woodpecker and is the *smallest woodpecker in* the region. Sometimes difficult to locate when feeding in thick bush or leafy canopy but its incessant tapping on a branch often reveals its position. Paler and less streaked below than the Golden-tailed Woodpecker, it has a *buff and yellow barred, not spotted back*. Flight action is fast and undulating. Frequents a wide range of habitats from thornveld to thick forests.

N. MYBURGH

Left: male

Rufous-naped Lark   *Mirafra africana*   15-18 cm

B. RYAN

 Most often seen during the breeding season when it perches on small bushes or termite mounds singing a simple 'treelee treelooe' phrase. Often flicks its wings during song phrase. It less regularly gives a display flight during which the song becomes jumbled chattering. Best recognized by its calls, combined with a *rufous nape and large rufous wing patches* which are conspicuous when the bird flushes. Found in open grasslands with stunted bushes, thornveld and agricultural lands.

Spike-heeled Lark   *Chersomanes albofasciata*   **13-15 cm**

J SOBEY

This small lark has an upright stance on long legs, and a long, slightly decurved bill. Its remarkably *short tail is black underneath and has a contrasting white tip* that is very noticeable in flight. The plumage varies from region to region but in general the bird shows *buffish underparts which contrast with a white throat*. It usually occurs in small groups. Found in grassland, scrub desert and desert gravel plains.

Sabota Lark   *Calendulauda sabota*   **15 cm**

L HES

A small, nondescript lark which has no obvious display flight or diagnostic song. Its habit of sitting on small trees and telephone wires and delivering its jumbled song full of mimicry are pointers to its identification. It has a short, thick bill, a buff or white eyebrow stripe which imparts a capped appearance, and it lacks the rufous wing patches seen in many other similar species. Frequents thornveld, open broadleafed woodland and scrub.

Red-capped Lark   *Calandrella cinerea* **14-15 cm**

N. MYBURGH

 A conspicuous and sometimes very common lark which gather in flocks outside the breeding season. Colour can vary from area to area but the combination of a *red cap and red shoulde smudges* are diagnostic. The underparts are *white to off-whi* and *clear*, unlike those of any other lark in the region. The call given b flocks in flight is a sparrow-like 'tchweerp'. Found in a wide range of hab itats from desert to moist grasslands.

Grey-backed Sparrowlark   *Eremopterix verticalis* **12-13 cm**

N. MYBURGH

Above: male
Below: female

N. MYBURGH

 This small grey and black bird is often flushed from road verges in the drier regions, especially the Karoo. When seen on the ground the diagnostic colouration of totally black underparts, greyish upperparts and black and white patterned head are clearly visible. The female is small and squat like the male, also has a pale conical bill and greyish upperparts, but has only a patch of black down the centre of the belly. Occurs mostly in small flocks when not breeding. Ranges from cultivated lands to scrub and true deserts.

Barn Swallow   *Hirundo rustica*   15-18 cm

W.R TARBOTON

Probably the most common swallow in the region between the months of November and March; before migrating in March large numbers are often seen *resting on telephone wires*. They roost in dense reedbeds, sometimes in hundreds of thousands. The ad. has a *brick red face and throat, a blue-black breast band* and off-white to buffish underparts. The tail streamers are very long and there are white spots on the tail base. Occurs over virtually any habitat; roosts in reedbeds.

Greater Striped Swallow   *Hirundo cucullata*   20 cm

W.R TARBOTON

Likely to be confused only with the Lesser Striped Swallow from which it is distinguished by being much *larger*, and by being far *paler* in overall appearance, with *faint striping* on white underparts discernible only at close range. The crown is pale orange and the *pale rufous on the rump* does not extend on to the vent. A common roadside bird in many areas especially near culverts, which it uses for breeding sites.

81

Lesser Striped Swallow   *Hirundo abyssinica* **15-17 cm**

A WILSON

Noticeably *smaller* than the Greater Striped Swallow, it diff(
in plumage by being *very heavily streaked on the underparts a*
by having a *rich rufous rump* which extends on to the vent.
also has a much richer rufous cap and nape. It occurs at low
altitudes than the Greater Striped Swallow and is frequently found in t
vicinity of buildings, on which it builds its nest.

South African Cliff-Swallow   *Hirundo spilodera* **15 cm**

N. MYBURGH

Might be confused with the Greater and the Lesser Strip(
swallows but this bird has only a *slightly notched tail*, is m(
rufous below with much reduced streaking, and has a *distin*
breast band. Has adapted to nesting under road bridges an
similar man-made structures and is commonly seen along the roadside
perched on wire fences.

Rock Martin   *Hirundo fuligula*   **12-15 cm**

 A medium-sized martin and the only one with *all-brown plumage*. It could be confused with the dark form of the Brown-throated Martin, but that species is smaller and shows a white belly and vent. The Rock Martin has the underparts slightly paler than the upperparts and, in flight, white spots are visible on the spread tail. It prefers rocky and mountainous terrain but has adapted to towns and cities, where it nests freely on buildings.

Red-breasted Swallow   *Hirundo semirufa*   **19-24 cm**

 This obviously *very large swallow* is readily identified by its conspicuous *rufous underparts* (diagnostic). In flight it can be seen that the red on the breast extends to the wing linings and forms a collar over the nape. The remainder of the plumage is a dark glossy blue and may appear black in some lights. It is usually encountered in pairs along roadsides or in mixed flocks of swallows. Found over open grassland in thornveld, and broadleafed woodland and upland grassland.

White-throated Swallow *Hirundo albigularis* 14-17 cm

ROY JOHANNESSON

The gleaming *white throat contrasts with the black breast band and greyish underparts*. A small red patch on the forehead is visible at close range. The remainder of the plumage is a glossy blue-black, and white spots are visible in the centre of the tail when the bird banks in flight. It is usually seen in pairs, generally near water, nesting under bridges and road culverts.

Black Cuckooshrike *Campephaga flava* 18-21 cm

J.L. VILJOEN

Male

W.G. McILLERON

Female

The male is an *all-black*, slightly glossy bird with an *inconspicuous yellow gape* and a more obvious *yellow shoulder* although the latter feature is not always present. The female is very different, *resembling a female cuckoo* with her *green and yellow barred plumage*, but is larger and has bright yellow outertail feathers. Unlike flycatchers and drongos, this bird creeps through foliage, gleaning insects from the undersides of leaves. Frequents a variety of woodlands from coastal forest to bushveld.

Fork-tailed Drongo   *Dicrurus adsimilis*   **23-26 cm**

A conspicuous and noisy bird which often perches freely in the open from where it hawks insects in flight or drops to the ground to retrieve food. It has a deeply forked tail and appears black all over, but in flight the underwing primaries can reflect light and the wing then appears pale edged. Fearless of large birds of prey, it frequently chases buzzards and even eagles, dive-bombing them from great heights. Inhabits a wide range of woodland, forest and open areas.

L. HES

Black-headed Oriole   *Oriolus larvatus*   **20-22 cm**

W.P. STANFORD

A bright, *golden-yellow bird* with *black head and throat, black wings* patched with white and bright coral-red bill. Females similar to males; imms. differ by having brownish head streaked with yellow and dull red bill. Although bright, remains well concealed in the leafy canopy. Difficult to detect unless fluty song or harsher 'kweeer' note is heard. Found in woodlands, bushveld and exotic plantations.

85

Cape Crow *Corvus capensis* **43-45 cm**

B. RYAN

The only *all-black crow* likely to be seen in the veld, far from human habitation. The *bill*, which is slightly decurved, is longer and *more pointed* than that of any other crow. At close range it can be seen that the plumage coloration ranges from oily black to glossy deep blues and purples. Pairs are usually seen sitting aloft some man-made structure, calling to each other and flicking their wings. Occurs in upland grasslands, open country, cultivated fields and arid regions.

House Crow *Corvus splendens* **34-38 cm**

J.C. SINCLAIR

A common and ever-increasing bird in Durban and Cape Town where it occurs in close association with the larger Pied Crow. Easily identified by its long thin body and tail, *dark grey body and black face, wings and tail*. A general scavenger in suburbia in coastal cities, occurring in small flocks but forming large roosts in trees in the evenings.

Pied Crow *Corvus albus* 46-50 cm

A. WEAVING

Unmistakable: the only crow in the region to have a *white belly*. Could possibly be confused with the White-necked Raven when seen in flight at long range but this species has a longer tail and a smaller, more compact head. Seldom seen in flocks unless attending a kill in a game reserve or roosting in trees near cities. Regular visitor to rubbish dumps.

White-necked Raven *Corvus albicollis* 54-56 cm

G. CUBITT

When seen at close range, the *massive black bill with a white tip and the white crescent on the nape* are diagnostic. In flight it is distinguished from other crows by its shape: large, heavy head, broad wings and a *short, broad tail*. Very aerodynamic, they often ride air currents in mountainous terrain, twisting and diving or chasing one another. The call is a very deep and throaty 'kwook'. Inhabits mountainous regions, open country and upland grasslands.

Southern Black Tit *Parus niger* **14-16 cm**

A typical tit in both behaviour and calls: its harsh chirring notes are often the first indication that a bird feeding party is in progress. The male and female are similar but the male is *more black*, less grey than the female and has a large area of *white in the wings* and white-tipped undertail coverts. Found in evergreen and coastal forest and thornveld.

H. VON HORSTEN

Left: male

Ashy Tit *Parus cinerascens* **13 cm**

N. MYBURGH

This small bird has a *slate grey body*, white-fringed wings, a *black cap, white cheeks, and a black throat and bib* extending as a black line down the belly. Very active; continually on the move through thickets, pecking and probing for food and regularly hanging upside down. Occasionally feeds on the ground where it hops about with a very upright stance. It travels in pairs or small parties, keeping in contact with a variety of ringing calls. Occurs in thornveld, broadleafed woodland and riverine scrub.

Arrow-marked Babbler *Turdoides jardineii* **21-24 cm**

 A very familiar bird in many parts of the region. This species habitually travels in groups, with members of the flock following one another, either feeding on the ground or flying up to trees. The birds keep up a constant soft chatter; however, if something alarms them, the *chatter builds into a crescendo*. Larger than a bulbul, this babbler appears generally drab brown but at close range the *arrow-like white markings* down the throat and breast and the *pale eye* are visible. Occurs in thornveld, broadleafed woodland and exotic plantations.

L. VON HORSTEN

Dark-Capped Bulbul *Pycnonotus tricolor* **19-22 cm**

H. VON HORSTEN

Probably one of the most familiar birds in most parts of the region as it has adapted successfully to cities and towns and commonly frequents gardens. Has a soft, unfeathered *black wattle around each eye*. This distinguishes it from the African Red-eyed Bulbul which has a red wattle. The more obvious features shared by these bulbuls are the *black head* and *bright yellow undertail coverts*. Occurs in thornveld, evergreen forests and is common in gardens.

Cape Bulbul *Pycnonotus capensis* **19-21 cm**

N. MYBURGH

Unlikely to be mistaken for the Dark-capped or Red-eyed Bulbul as the ranges do not overlap, and this species is easily identified by its *conspicuous white eye wattle*. It is also a much darker bird having the dark head colour extending well on to the breast and belly. Is less confiding and not as habituated to man as other bulbuls. Inhabits fynbos, coastal scrub, riverine forests and exotic plantations.

African Red-eyed Bulbul *Pycnonotus nigricans* **19-21 cm**

J.J. BROOKS

Easily distinguished from the Cape and Dark-capped bulbuls by its diagnostic *red eye wattles*. Other less obvious differences are a *darker head* and an overall *slightly paler appearance*. The ranges of these three bulbuls rarely overlap; this species i found in the more arid regions where it is a common bird around water holes. Its call is a liquid 'cheloop chreeep choop' and a shorter 'kwit-kwit' alarm note. An inhabitant of river courses in dry thornveld and scrub areas.

90

Kurrichane Thrush   *Turdus libonyanus* **18-22 cm**

N. BRICKELL

Often shy in its natural environment, this bird has adapted to parks and gardens in many areas and become bold, venturing out on to open lawns in search of food. When disturbed it will fly up into a tree and sit motionless until the intruder has passed. It closely resembles the Olive Thrush but has a *bright orange bill* and a speckled white throat with obvious *black moustachial stripes*. Alarm call is a distinct 'peet-peeooo'. Frequents thornveld, open woodland and parks and gardens.

Olive Thrush   *Turdus olivaceus* **20-22 cm**

N. MYBURGH

In many respects the Olive Thrush is very similar to the Kurrichane Thrush but it has a *yellow bill*, a *dusky speckled throat* and lacks the black moustachial stripes. Forages in leaf litter but it will also take berries and fruit. Early in the morning it gives a rich, melodic song which is a variation on a whistled 'wheet-tooo-weet' phrase. Occurs in evergreen forests, coastal scrub, and parks and gardens.

Cape Rock-Thrush *Monticola rupestris* **19-21 cm**

A fairly shy and unobtrusive bird of rocky hillsides, it sometimes ventures into picnic sites where it becomes bold, picking up food scraps. The male is easily identified by his entirely blue head which contrasts with the orange breast. The female is duller being a rusty red on the head and body. The male often perches on a rock or boulder, with the bill pointing skywards, and gives his soft whistled song. Frequents mountainous and rocky terrain, both at the coast and inland.

Above: male
Above right: female

Groundscraper Thrush *Psophocichla litsitsirupa* **22-24 cm**

Much bolder than other thrushes and is frequently seen hopping around in parks and gardens and at picnic sites in game reserves. When foraging on the ground it often raises a wing, as if saluting, revealing a *contrasting black and white pattern on the underwing*. Has a very upright stance and this, combined with the *bold facial markings* and the *heavily spotted breast*, makes identification easy. The song is a clearly whistled phrase. Found in dry thornveld, open broadleafed woodland, and parks and gardens.

Mountain Wheatear *Oenanthe monticola* 18-20 cm

J J BROOKS

J J BROOKS

Above: male
Right: female

When driving over mountain passes or through rocky arid areas, the startling black and white bird which flushes from the road-side is most likely to be this species. Very flighty and nervous, it will not allow close approach but the very obvious *black and white pied plumage* should render it unmistakable. It could be confused with the male Stonechat but the latter is much smaller and has a rufous breast. Some males are greyish instead of black but all show a *white cap, shoulder patch and rump*. The female is greyish and nondescript but also shows the diagnostic white rump. Inhabits mountainous and rocky terrain.

Capped Wheatear *Oenanthe pileata* 17-18 cm

ROY JOHANNESSON

A bird of the open level veld with little grass cover and plenty of termite mounds to use as look-out posts. It has a very upright posture at rest. It can run very rapidly and, when it flies, its *white rump and sides of the tail* are conspicuous. The *white eye-brow stripe, black cap and black collar* are diagnostic. In display, the male hovers over the female and his territory and gives his jumbled warbling song. Found in barren sandy or stony areas and in short grasslands.

Familiar Chat *Cercomela familiaris* **14-15 cm**

A small, dark greyish-brown bird which lacks any obvious fie
characters except its behaviour. Most small chats have the hab
of nervously *flicking their wings* slightly open, which exposes t
rump and uppertail which are normally boldly patterned: th
Familiar Chat continually performs this *wing-flicking motion*, and displays
russet rump and outertail feathers. It inhabits rocky and mountainous te
rain, and open woodland in some areas.

Anteating Chat *Myrmecocichla formicivora* **17-18 cm**

Associated with the open veld and termite mounds on which
perches with an upright posture to scan its territory. Alwa
occurs in pairs or small parties and is very active, taking sh
flights, hopping across the veld or *hovering into the wind* befo
darting off downwind. Appears black but at close range its rich *chocola
brown plumage* can be seen. Some males have a *white shoulder patch* but
birds show *white 'windows' in the wing tips*, a feature visible only in fligh

African Stonechat   *Saxicola torquatus*   **13-14 cm**

A small chat, the male of which has conspicuous plumage of a *black head*, bright white sides to the neck, a *rufous chest, white patches in the wings and a white rump*, all of which are very obvious in flight. The female is far drabber, lacking the black head and having rusty brown plumage but she also shows a white rump. Almost always occurs in pairs and is common in many areas; has adapted to the canefields of KwaZulu-Natal. The call, a 'weeet' followed by a harsh 'chaaak' sounds like two stones being tapped together, hence its name. Inhabits upland grasslands, open treeless areas with short scrub, and sugarcane plantations.

N. MYBURGH

L. VON HORSTEN

Above right: male
Right: female

Red-Capped Robin-Chat   *Cossypha natalensis*   **16-18 cm**

N. BRICKELL

This small forest robin is extremely shy and furtive, preferring to keep to the darker tangles of thickets in evergreen forests where, during the day, it forages in leaf litter. At dusk and dawn it becomes more confiding and will enter open areas at the forest edge to feed. The bright *orange-red plumage with powder-blue wings* is diagnostic. The normal call is a frequently repeated 'see-saw' note.

Cape Robin-Chat *Cossypha caffra* **16-17 cm**

N. MYBURGH

This shy robin is easily recognized by its *short white eyebrow stripe and by having the orange coloration confined to the throat and upper breast.* It feeds mostly on the ground but creeps up through vegetation and sits on an exposed perch to sing. Imm is mottled and spotted buff but shows a *reddish tail with a dark centre.* Song is a short warbled phrase and the alarm call is a harsh 'grrrr'. Frequent montane river valley scrub, evergreen forests and fynbos.

White-browed Scrub-Robin *Cercotrichas leucophrys* **14-16 cm**

A. WILSON

A bird which is heard more often than seen, as it sings from deep within a bush. The song is very variable but the usual phrase is a short 'tchweet-chereee-wheeet'. The bird has diagnostic *heavy streaking down the breast, a white eyebrow stripe and white spots in the wing* which form a white wing bar. The tail tip is spotted white; the tail is frequently raised and lowered, displaying the russet rump. Found in both dry and moist broadleafed woodland, thornveld and forest.

White-browed Robin-Chat *Cossypha heuglini* **19-20 cm**

A. WEAVING

An explosive rush of melodious and repetitive song from thick, tangled scrub early in the morning often indicates the presence of this species. It is furtive but, if seen, the *red-orange underparts*, and dark head with a *broad white eyebrow stripe* soon identify the bird. The imm. is drabber than the ad. and has buff-tipped feathers on the mantle and back. Occurs in dense riverine thickets and tangles, and parks and gardens.

Karoo Scrub-Robin *Cercotrichas coryphoeus* **14-17 cm**

This small greyish bird is common in the fynbos of the south and west and in the more arid regions. It is easily recognized if flushed as the *black tail*, which is held *fanned in flight*, shows a *conspicuous white tip*. The overall plumage is *drab grey, slightly paler below, and there is a short white eyebrow stripe* and a russet base to the tail. It feeds on the ground, hopping about with its tail cocked; it dashes for cover when disturbed. It perches on small shrubs to deliver the short, jumbled song. Frequents semi-arid scrub and fynbos.

A. WEAVING

Chestnut-vented Tit-Babbler *Parisoma subcaeruleum* 14-15 c

N. MYBURGH

Most often seen as it creeps through thick thorn bush deliver its loud, explosive song. It is a *greyish bird with a longish t chestnut vent* (diagnostic), and a pale eye. The folded wing sho a *chequered shoulder* and the *throat is streaked black*. The son rendered as a liquid 'cheruuup-chee-chee', interspersed with harsher ch tering notes. Occurs mostly in pairs which maintain contact through th fluty calls. Inhabits dry thornveld, thickets and dry scrub in arid regions.

Lesser Swamp-Warbler *Acrocephalus gracilirostris* 14-16 cm

B. RYAN

A confusing variety of small birds frequents thick stands of ree and this warbler is one of them. It is relatively common and present throughout the year. It appears much like any oth drab warbler but is *fairly large* and has *brownish upperparts an clearer white underparts* than similar warblers. Often seen low down on th edge of reedbeds, flitting among the stems, collecting insects from th water's surface. Its *liquid, melodious song* is heard from reedbeds. Frequent reedbeds adjoining wetlands.

Little Rush-Warbler *Bradypterus baboecala* **13-16 cm**

N MYBURGH

Dark brown with a long tail, if glimpsed this bird resembles a rodent as it scuttles close to the base of reed stems. When displaying during the breeding season the male gives a series of fast 'brrrup' call notes and performs a short *fluttery flight among the reeds or just above them.* During the flight the *short rounded wings and long heavy tail* are noticeable. It also gives a catlike mewing call. Inhabits reedbeds adjoining dams, lagoons and large rivers.

Bar-throated Apalis *Apalis thoracica* **11-12 cm**

J J BROOKS

This *small, long-tailed bird* is easily identified by its *greyish or greenish upperparts, creamy underparts with a thin, dark bar across the breast* and a pale, creamy eye. It might be mistaken for the Yellow-breasted Apalis but lacks any yellow on the breast. Occurs in pairs in forest or scrub and creeps through the midstratum or low down, gleaning insects or caterpillars from under leaves. The song is a rapidly repeated 'pillip-pillip'. Frequents evergreen and coastal forests, scrub and fynbos.

Yellow-breasted Apalis *Apalis flavida* **11-12 cm**

Male

Apalises are lively, *long-tailed warblers*, continually on the move in forest or bush and, although many of them remain high in the canopy, this species prefers the lower or midstratum. It can be identified by the combination of a *greyish cap, white throat and bright yellow breast* which, in the male, has a *small black bar* on the lower breast. The call is a fast, buzzy 'chizzek-chizzek' which is repeated frequently. Occurs in thornveld and broadleafed woodland.

Long-billed Crombec *Sylvietta rufescens* **12 cm**

A small greyish bird with *buffy cinnamon underparts, this species appears almost tailless*. It is easily distinguished from similar warblers as the bill is long and noticeably decurved. This active bird occurs in pairs or small groups and is a regular attendant at bird parties. It feeds by gleaning insects from branches and leaves and will probe crevices with its long bill. The call is a frequently repeated 'tree-trriit'. Occurs in a wide range of woodlands and semi-arid scrub; avoids moist forests.

Green-backed Camaroptera   *Camaroptera brachyura* **10-11 cm**

N. MYBURGH

This species resembles the well-known Wren of the northern hemisphere. It keeps low down in thick vegetation and habitually *cocks its tail*. It has *off-white to greyish underparts*. When excited or disturbed, it will flit through the undergrowth giving a metallic clicking sound but the normal call is a loud, snapping 'bidup-bidup-bidup'. Found in moist evergreen forests, dry broadleafed woodland and thornveld. This warbler is replaced by the Grey-backed Camaroptera in the dry western parts of the region.

Zitting Cisticola   *Cisticola juncidis* **10 cm**

N. MYBURGH

Cisticolas are notoriously difficult to identify and the Zitting is no exception unless the bird is calling or displaying. It is a tiny bird with a finely streaked forehead and well-marked buff and black back. The tail, which is short and often held fanned, has a dark subterminal band and a white tip. In its display flight, the bird *flies around* at no great height in a bounding, erratic manner, *continually giving its 'zit-zit-zit-zit' call*. It occurs in grasslands, preferring damp or marshy areas.

Grey-backed Cisticola *Cisticola subruficapilla* 13-14 cm

This, the common cisticola in fynbos and arid Karoo scrub, is *long-tailed* and has a *grey-streaked back and chestnut cap*. For most of the year it is unobtrusive and skulks in scrub but when breeding it becomes obvious with its aerial display and calls. The call, a loud, muffled 'prrrttt' followed by sharp 'phweee-phweee-phweee' notes, is given in a fluttery low flight over its territory. It is found in fynbos, grassy hillsides and desert scrub.

N. MYBURGH

Rattling Cisticola *Cisticola chiniana* 11-14 cm

The most abundant cisticola of the thornveld and probably the most conspicuous of all the cisticolas. It perches openly on the tops of bushes and proclaims its territory with a *loud 'chureee-chureee'* song, that ends with a *rattling 'cherrrr'*. When one is walking through the bush, this is the small, long-tailed bird with a chestnut cap which approaches and boldly scolds with a consistent 'cheee-cheee' alarm note. Frequents thornveld, broadleafed woodland and the edge of coastal forest.

B.C. HARMSE

Karoo Prinia *Prinia maculosa* **12-14 cm**

P. PICKFORD

The common prinia found in low scrub and bracken and briar habitat in the fynbos, Karoo and some mountainous areas. Unlikely to be confused with other prinias or cisticolas because of the *diagnostic streaking on its breast*. Like other prinias, it has a long tail which is often held cocked at right angles. An easily agitated bird often seen perched on a grass stem giving its sharp 'chleet-chleet-chleet' call.

Marico Flycatcher *Bradornis mariquensis* **18 cm**

L. VON HÖRSTEN

A nondescript flycatcher which has *uniform dun brown upperparts* and *clear white underparts*. At close range a buffish ring around the eye and a buff panel in the wings are discernible. At rest, the bird appears very *white breasted and has an upright stance*. It uses prominent perches from which it hawks insects; it often returns to the same perch. Occurs in pairs and small groups and is a common roadside bird in mixed thornveld and dry broadleafed woodland in the drier north-western regions.

Fiscal Flycatcher *Sigelus silens* **17-20 cm**

Male   **Female**

This bird resembles a Common Fiscal but it has a *shorter tail* with *obvious white patches on either side, it lacks white on the shoulders* and has a short, fine bill and not the thick hooked bill of a shrike. Its habits also differ in that it behaves like a flycatcher and does not sit in such exposed situations as the Fiscal Shrike. The imm. is brown, not black. Occurs singly or in pairs and is normally silent. Inhabits fynbos, mountainous scrub and open broadleafed woodland.

Cape Batis *Batis capensis* **13 cm**

A large and chunky batis. The male shows *russet over the wings and flanks* as well as a broad black breast band; the female might be mistaken for the Chinspot Batis but has the *russet breast band extending down the sides of the breast and over the flanks*. It occurs in pairs and in bird parties and is an active flycatcher in the mid-canopy. Found in moist evergreen forest and heavily wooded gorges in mountainous areas.

Chinspot Batis   *Batis molitor* 13 cm

Male

Female

A small black and white flycatcher, the female of which has a *broad chestnut breast band* and a diagnostic *chestnut spot on the chin*. The male lacks the chestnut spot and its *breast band is black*. Normally occurs in pairs. Will glean insects from foliage as well as hawk flies, which it does with an audible snap of the bill. Call note is a clear, whistled 'teuu-teuu-teuu' and harsher 'chrr-chrr-chrr' notes. Occurs in dry broadleafed woodland and thornveld.

African Paradise-Flycatcher   *Terpsiphone viridis* 20 + 18 cm tail in ♂

The male African Paradise-Flycatcher is unmistakable. It has an *extraordinarily long tail* which, like the back, is rufous and contrasts with the blue-grey underparts and darker head. The female and imm. lack the very long tail. An active and noisy bird, whose harsh 'tic-tic-chaa-chaa' notes are often heard before the bird is seen. Dashes about in the mid-canopy chasing insects, rarely settling at one perch for very long. Frequents a wide range of woodland habitats.

Male   **Female**

African Pied Wagtail   *Motacilla aguimp*   **20 cm**

A. WILSON

Unmistakable and unlikely to be confused with any other species in the region. The *black and white plumage*, combined with the *long tail which is continually bobbed* up and down, is diagnostic. The female has a sootier breast band than the male. Feeds on the ground, usually in damp areas close to water, but may be found far from water. Dashes to and fro chasing insects, its tail busily moving up and down. Call is a 'chee-cheroo'.

Cape Wagtail   *Motacilla capensis*   **19-20 cm**

RAYMONDE JOHANNESSON

A much dowdier bird than the African Pied Wagtail, with the black being replaced by *greyish-brown which sometimes has an olive wash*. Habits very similar to those of the African Pied Wagtail, with much running around and *tail wagging* when chasing insects. Prefers damp and marshy areas but will frequent watered grassy lawns in parks and gardens. When not breeding, large flocks may gather to form communal roosts in trees.

African Pipit *Anthus cinnamomeus* 16-17 cm

A. WILSON

The pipit most likely to be seen in the open veld or grasslands near towns and cities. It is fairly nondescript: *buff and brown* with *streaking on the breast*, and *prominent white outertail feathers* visible in flight. Always feeds on the ground where it runs short distances, stops to pick up food and then stands with a very upright posture. In display flight the bird flies high in a series of bounding loops, finally plummeting in a spiral with its wings held over its back.

Cape Longclaw *Macronyx capensis* 20 cm

A. WEAVING

Most often encountered when flushed in the veld: in flight the tail is usually held spread, showing the white tips, and the flight is on stiffly held wings which are kept spread below body level. The back is well streaked and mottled. Only on landing, and when the bird is facing the viewer, can the brilliant orange throat, surrounded by a black band and duller orange-yellow underparts, be seen. The call is a cat-like mewing and a loud whistled 'cheeruup'. Occurs in coastal and upland grasslands.

107

Yellow-throated Longclaw *Macronyx croceus* 20-22 cm

J. SOBEY

A long-legged and long-toed bird of grasslands which has a proportionately *short, white-tipped tail* which is conspicuous in flight. The underparts are *bright canary-yellow and there is a broad black gorget*. When flushed, the bird flies with jerky wing beats and glides with its tail spread, showing the white tips. It frequently alights on the top of a bush and utters its loud, whistling 'phooooeeet' call. Found in grasslands adjoining wetlands, coastal lagoons and estuaries.

Common Fiscal *Lanius collaris* 21-23 cm

ROY JOHANNESSON

ROY JOHANNESSON

Superficially resembles the Fiscal Flycatcher but is more robust in build, has a much longer tail and has *white shoulder patches*. It also has a more powerful bill which is obviously hooked. The female has a *rufous patch on the flanks* and the imm. is mottled brown above and has grey barring below. A common and familiar bird, which hunts from perches in exposed situations. When perched, it often holds its tail at an angle to the body. Found in a wide range of habitats but avoids dense forests.

Above left: male
Left: female

Red-backed Shrike *Lanius collurio* 16-18 cm

Male

Female

A small, colourful shrike which has a *grey head and rump, black mask* through the eye, a black tail and very conspicuous *chestnut back and wings*. The female is drab brown above with a pale eye-stripe and fine brown barring on the underparts. A typical shrike, it perches in exposed positions from where it can scan the ground or the insects on which it feeds. It also skulks and, when disturbed, will retire to thickets to hide. Found in broadleafed woodland and thornveld.

Southern Boubou *Laniarius ferrugineus* 20-22 cm

Although it resembles a Common Fiscal, the Southern Boubou is unlikely to be mistaken for the former species because of its very different habits. It is difficult to see as it keeps well hidden in deep tangles in the undergrowth and rarely ventures into the open. When glimpsed, the impression is of a *black and russet bird with a white wing bar*. The female has slaty grey, not black upperparts, and is more rufous below than the male. The call is often heard as members of a pair keep contact by duetting a 'booo-booo' followed by a 'whee-ooo', and variations on this. It is found in dense thickets in riverine and evergreen forests.

Above left: male
Left: female

109

Crimson-breasted Shrike *Laniarius atrococcineus* **23 cm**

Unmistakable: one of the most startlingly coloured birds of dry bushveld. The brilliant *crimson underparts* contrast with *jet black upperparts* which are offset by a *white flash down wing*. Although very brightly coloured, it can be difficult to as it tends to skulk in the undergrowth. However, it often feeds on ground and sometimes in fairly open areas. The call is an unusual clonk sound and a harsh 'grrr'. Found in thornveld and dry river courses.

Black-backed Puffback *Dryoscopus cubla* **16-18 cm**

Female

This small shrike is a noisy and conspicuous member of b parties foraging in the mid- and top canopy. The male has a *black cap and obvious red eye, a grey and black back* and a gnostic *white rump*. In display, the male fluffs his rump feath into a *fur-like white ball* and dashes through the foliage in pursuit of female. The female is paler than the male. They have a variety of con calls. Frequents a wide range of woodland and forest.

Black-crowned Tchagra   *Tchagra senegalus*   **19-22 cm**

 This species is shy and furtive and when flushed from cover will fly quickly to the next bush, briefly showing its *chestnut wings and white-tipped black tail*. Only when the diagnostic *black line down the centre of the crown* is seen can a positive identification be made. It sometimes feeds on the ground but mostly is seen as it moves through the lower tangles of bush. The whistled crescendo of this shrike is a typical bushveld sound. Occurs in mixed thornveld and riverine scrub.

Bokmakierie   *Telophorus zeylonus*   **22-23 cm**

 This robust shrike is a familiar bird in many areas and its call is commonly heard. The ad. is easily recognized by its *grey head, green back and bright yellow underparts with a black gorget*. The imm. lacks the black gorget, but the undertail, like that of the ad., has conspicuous yellow tips which are obvious in flight. Display consists of head bowing and tail raising by both adults as they face each other. Found in fynbos, Karoo scrub and scrub-filled valleys in mountainous areas.

White-Crested Helmet-Shrike   *Prionops plumatus* 17-20 cm

Always seen in small groups flitting through open woodland i follow-my-leader style. Flocks are conspicuous when they tak flight as they show their *pied black and white plumage with a la of white in the wings and tail*. At rest the bird shows a *grey cres white collar*, clear white underparts and a black tail. The *yellow eye wattl* is noticeable at close range. Found in mixed woodlands and thornveld.

Common Starling   *Sturnus vulgaris* 20-22 cm

Non-breeding

During the breeding season the ad. is an *iridescent green, blue and black* but appears all black when not seen in sunlight, anc the bill is bright yellow. The non-breeding bird is conspicuously spotted with white and has a dark bill, while the imm. is browr and has a paler throat. Sometimes occurs in large flocks, especially wher roosting or feeding in fields. Song is a bubbling jumble of squeaks anc mimicry. Occurs in cities, towns and farmlands.

Common Myna *Acridotheres tristis* **25 cm**

P. PICKFORD

A starling-sized bird which, in flight, shows conspicuous *white patches in the wings and a white-tipped tail*. At rest it appears brown with a glossy black head, a *bright yellow bill, bare yellow skin around the eyes*, and yellow legs. A noisy inhabitant of cities and towns where it feeds on open lawns and fields and along roadsides. Gathers in large roosts in the evenings and is generally considered a pest.

Pied Starling *Spreo bicolour* **27-28 cm**

L. VON HORSTEN

This large, dark brown, almost black starling is readily identified by its *conspicuous white vent and undertail coverts*. At closer range the pale eye and the *yellow base to the bill* are noticeable. It feeds on the ground, often among livestock, and will search for ectoparasites on animals' backs. Forms large flocks in the early morning and evening, flying at considerable height to and from the roosting areas. The call is a loud 'skeeer-kerrra-kerrra'. Occurs in open grasslands and areas under cultivation.

Wattled Starling *Creatophora cinerea* **19-21 cm**

Breeding male   **Non-breeding**

In flight appears similar to the imm. Common Starling but Wattled Starling has a *pale rump*. A greyish bird with black w *and tail*, during the breeding season the male attains wa and becomes very conspicuous, showing his *black and ye patterned head*. When breeding, this species forms large colonies which in trees and bushes. Has a sharp 'sreeeeo' call note. Found in grassla thornveld and broadleafed woodlands.

Violet-backed Starling *Cinnyricinclus leucogaster* **15-17 cm**

Above: male
Below: female

The male of this sma starling is an unusual *glossy amethyst colou on the head, throat a upperparts* but, at a distance, it appears black and white. The female is very different: *her drab brown upperparts and heavily streaked underparts* impart a thrush-like appearance. This species is seen in pairs or small groups in trees, rarely on the ground. The call is a short 'tip-tip-tip'. Inhabits moist woodlands and thornveld; avoids evergreen forests.

Cape Glossy Starling   *Lamprotornis nitens*   **25 cm**

The *iridescent coloration* of this bird is evident only in direct sunlight; at a distance, it *can appear black*. The bright orange eye is wide, staring and button-like. There are two rows of black spots on the wing coverts and the bird can be distinguished from the Black-bellied Starling by its brighter glossy plumage and by having an *iridescent greenish-blue, not black belly*. It occurs in pairs or small parties and does not normally form large flocks. Found in thornveld, mixed woodlands and suburbia.

Black-bellied Starling   *Lamprotornis corruscus*   **18-21 cm**

P. PICKFORD

Resembles the Cape Glossy Starling but is less glossy, with a *matt black belly and flanks*, and has a yellow, not orange eye. It is also noticeably smaller and more slender than the Cape Glossy Starling and has a proportionately longer tail. It frequently forms large flocks out of the breeding season and is much noisier and more demonstrative than the Glossy Starling. Occurs in coastal and riverine forests in the east.

Red-winged Starling   *Onychognathus morio* **27-30 cm**

Above: male
Below: female

This *large, long-tailed starling* is easily recognized in flight when the bright *chestnut primaries* can clearly be seen; at rest, the chestnut is not normally visible on the folded wing. The male is a slightly glossy dark blue, while the female is duller, with a dark grey head and breast but she still shows the chestnut primaries. Sometimes occurs in large flocks. Call is a whistled and often mournful 'cherleeeoo' or 'pee-yoo' Inhabits rocky ravines, and cliffs; has adapted to suburbia.

Red-billed Oxpecker   *Buphagus erythrorhynchus* **19-21 cm**

This species is usually seen peering over the back of a large mammal and giving its scolding 'chrrr' call note and a hissing 'zzzzzzzist'. As it scrambles over the animal's body looking for ticks, the *large red bill* and the *bare yellow skin around the ey* are clearly visible. Young birds have a dark bill with a yellow base. When no feeding, small groups sit around in trees or fly between herds with their starling-like flight. Occurs in thornveld and broadleafed woodland.

Cape Sugarbird   *Promerops cafer*   ♂=34-44 cm ♀=25-29 cm

 The male is an easily identified bird with its combination of an *extremely long and wispy tail, long decurved bill, greyish-brown upperparts and speckled drab underparts with a bright lemon vent* and undertail coverts. The female and imm. are similar to the male and although they have long tails, these are never quite as long as the male's. In courtship and display the male dances in mid-air with wings flapping vigorously and his long tail partially spread as he repeatedly flicks it over his back. Found in fynbos, particularly in stands of proteas.

Above left: male
Left: female

Malachite Sunbird   *Nectarinia famosa*   ♂ =25 cm ♀ =15 cm

Male   G. CUBITT   **Female**   ROY JOHANNESSON

 The *largest sunbird* in the region and the only one with an *all-metallic green plumage with long tail projections*. The male in 'eclipse' plumage loses his green sheen for a short period and then resembles the female. The female is olive-brown above and has yellowish underparts but is distinguished by her large size and long, decurved bill. The male's call is a high-pitched ringing 'zing-zing'. Occurs in fynbos, protea- and aloe-covered slopes, and mountain scrub.

Orange-breasted Sunbird   *Anthobaphes violacea*   ♂ =15 cm ♀ =12 c

Male   **Female**

 The only small sunbird in the region to have pointed tail projections. The head is an iridescent green and blue, the back a dull olive, and the *breast and belly bright orange*. In the fynbos habitat, the female could be confused only with the female Southern Double-collared Sunbird but is noticeably larger and is a more uniform olive-green above and below. When breeding, the male makes himself conspicuous by sitting on an exposed perch and singing his short buzzy song. Inhabits fynbos and flowering aloe stands.

Marico Sunbird   *Cinnyris mariquensis*   11-13,5 cm

Male   **Female**

 Unlike many other sunbirds that have scarlet bands across the breast, the male of this species has an *iridescent purple band* that contrasts with the black belly. The head and back are a metallic iridescent greenish-blue and the bill is long and decurved. The female is a drab olive-brown above with paler, streaked underparts and poses complex identification problems with many other similar female sunbirds; however, her long, robust and decurved bill is the distinguishing feature. Frequents thornveld and dry broadleafed woodland.

118

Male   Female

The *smallest of the sunbirds that have a scarlet breast band*. Confusion arises with the Greater Double-collared Sunbird from which it can be distinguished by its *smaller size, shorter and finer decurved bill, and a much narrower scarlet breast band*. The emale differs from the female Greater Double-collared Sunbird by the maller bill character and from the female Orange-breasted Sunbird by being greyer on the underparts. The call is a harsh 'chee-chee'. Found in oastal scrub, fynbos and forest edge.

ireater Double-collared Sunbird *Cinnyris afer* 14 cm

Male   Female

Within its range likely to be confused only with the Southern Double-collared Sunbird from which it can be distinguished as it is considerably *larger*, has a *longer, thicker bill and a broader scarlet breast band*. The females of both species are olive and lark brown but the female Greater Double-collared is noticeably greener on the underparts and has a longer, heavier bill. It is active and restless, flitng about and uttering a harsh 'tchut-tchut-tchut'. Occurs in stands of proeas and aloes in mountainous terrain.

White-bellied Sunbird *Cinnyris talatala* **11 cm**

Left: male
Above: female

A very small sunbird and the only one in the region to have a *bottle green head and back, and a white belly*. The female is non-descript and looks like a small grey warbler with a white belly, but the long decurved bill confirms that it is a sunbird. The male is conspicuous during the breeding season when he perches high to deliver his fast, buzzy song. At other times, they keep to forest edge and thicket.

Scarlet-chested Sunbird *Chalcomitra senegalensis* **15 cm**

Male
Female

A large, chunky sunbird, the male is unmistakable: it has a *matt black body and bright scarlet breast*. At close range the iridescent blue flecks on the scarlet breast can be seen. The female resembles the female Amethyst Sunbird but has *more mottled underparts* and *lacks the buff moustachial stripes* of that species. The male is bold and conspicuous, chasing other birds from his territory. The song is a loud 'cheeup-chup-toop-toop' whistle. Occurs in mixed dry and moist woodland, thornveld, and suburbia.

120

Amethyst Sunbird   *Chalcomitra amethystina*   **15 cm**

Although this sunbird is the same length as the Scarlet-chested Sunbird, it is more *slender* and has a neater, more compact body shape. This appearance, together with its longer tail, should help in identifying the confusingly similar females of these two species. The male is easily distinguished by his *matt black plumage* which is relieved only by an *iridescent greenish-violet patch on the throat and shoulder, and a bronze-green forehead*. These patches are not easy to see unless the bird is in direct sunlight. The female closely resembles the female Scarlet-chested Sunbird but has very obvious buff moustachial stripes and is paler and less streaked below. Found in evergreen, coastal and riverine forest, and suburbia.

Above left: male
Left: female

Cape White-eye   *Zosterops capensis*   **12 cm**

ROY JOHANNESSON

The plumage of this warbler-like bird varies from region to region but it is usually *olive-green above, greyish below* and has a diagnostic *ring of white feathering around the eye*. They are noisy and active birds, commonly found in groups as they work their way through the undergrowth or high canopy. They are inveterate members of bird parties and the soft 'tweee-tuuu-twee-twee' call is continually repeated as they keep contact. Found in a wide range of habitats, including gardens.

Red-billed Buffalo-Weaver   *Bubalornis niger*   21-24 cm

N. BRICKELL

Male

The only large, *black, sparrow-like bird* in the region. It has a robust red bill and in flight shows white patches in the primary feathers. The female and imm. are browner versions of the male. Feeds mostly on the ground; when disturbed, groups will fly up into trees. Their nests are large, untidy bundles of thorny sticks, placed in trees and windmills. Occurs in dry thornveld and broadleafed woodland.

White-browed Sparrow-Weaver   *Plocepasser mahali*   17-19 cm

A. WEAVING

A plump, short-tailed bird with a *broad white eyebrow stripe which runs from behind the eye, a conspicuous white rump* (visible in flight), and a white wing stripe. It occurs in groups, usually near the nesting or roosting trees. The nests, many of which are placed in a single tree, are untidy bundles of straw. The birds' loud and liquid 'cheeoop-preeoo-chop' call is given from these colonies; a harsher 'chik-chik' alarm call is also given. Found in thornveld and dry, scrubby river courses.

ouse Sparrow   *Passer domesticus*   **14 cm**

ale   **Female**

W. G. McILLERON

N. MYBURGH

Its close association with man makes this possibly the best known bird in the region. The male has a grey crown and rump, black bib, pale cheeks, chestnut mantle and a white wing bar. The female is a drab greyish-brown with a streaked mantle, a ffish eyebrow stripe and paler off-white underparts. A displaying male ll droop his wings, cock his tail and hold his head back as he hops around female. Rarely absent from human habitation; has colonized remote rms and offshore islands of the region.

ape Sparrow   *Passer melanurus*   **15 cm**

ale   **Female**

ROY JOHANNESSON

ROY JOHANNESSON

A larger and plumper bird than the House Sparrow, the male is also more distinctively marked with a *bold black and white head pattern*. The female has a chestnut mantle and a shadow impression of the male's head pattern. It has adapted to human abitation but is frequently found in remote areas, far from urban devel-oment. Occurs mostly in small groups or pairs but at times forms large ocks and joins parties of bishops, weavers and queleas feeding on old ain fields and crops.

123

Southern Grey-headed Sparrow *Passer diffusus* **15 cm**

An unobtrusive sparrow which has a *grey head and underparts*, *a chestnut mantle and rump*, and a *white wing bar*. Might be mistaken for the female House Sparrow but the very obvious grey head should eliminate confusion. Occurs in the vicinity of farm buildings and yards where it associates with Cape and House Sparrow but it is more often seen in open woodland, particularly on dead trees in which it can nest. Occurs in mixed woodland and suburbia in some areas.

Yellow-throated Petronia *Petronia superciliaris* **15 cm**

Frequently mistaken for White-browed Sparrow-Weaver because of the *broad buffy eyebrow stripe* which begins just above the eye and can appear very white in some lights and plumages. However, the Yellow-throated Petronia is very much smaller, lacks a white rump and has buff underparts. This species can also resemble a female House Sparrow but its eyebrow stripe is broader, it has two buff wing bars and would seldom be found in the same habitat. Occurs in small groups. Inhabits thornveld, broadleafed woodland and riverine bush.

W R TARBOTON

W P STANFORD

Scaly-feathered Finch *Sporopipes squamifrons* **10 cm**

 When in flight, this tiny finch appears as a grey blur but, when seen at rest, the contrasting *black and white malar stripes, freckled black and white forehead and white fringed wing and tail feathers* make identification easy. It feeds mostly on the ground and it is not easy to see but when flushed it will settle on bushes in an exposed position. The call is an indistinct 'chizz-chizz' given by birds in flight. Found in dry thornveld, and at cattle enclosures, watering troughs and around farm buildings.

Thick-billed Weaver *Amblyospiza albifrons* **15-17 cm**

Male

Female

 This large weaver is the only one with such a *massive, thick bill,* and *dark brown plumage relieved only by white patches in the wings* and a *white forehead*. The female appears markedly different, being brown above and paler and heavily streaked below, but still shows the large bill. Small flocks are often seen as they fly to and from their roosts, giving their 'tweek-tweek' call. In flight, the males' white wing patches appear translucent. Occurs in evergreen and coastal forests, and in reedbeds.

Village Weaver   *Ploceus cucullatus*   14-16 cm

The male in breeding plumage is the *only black-faced weaver to have a yellow and bla␣ speckled back*. The race that occu␣ in the north has the same extent of black on the head as the Southern Masked-Weaver but the spotted back should help distinguish the species. When not breeding the male loses his brigh␣ yellow plumage and attains the drab greenish and olive colour of the female and imm. It is then exceedingly difficult to differenti-ate from other weavers in similar plumage. Breeds, sometimes in large colonies, in trees overhang-ing water.

L. HES

P. PICKFORD

Above left: breeding male
Left: female

Cape Weaver   *Ploceus capensis*   17 cm

ROY JOHANNESSON

Most likely to be con-fused with the Yellow Weaver from which it distinguished by bein␣ larger, less brilliant yellow in colour, having an *orange- or rust-coloured wash over the face, and ␣ having a cream, not red eye*. The non-breeding male resembles the olive and yellowish female and imm. The breeding colonies are usually situated in reedbeds or ir␣ trees overhanging water. The ma␣ will hang from a completed nest and sway from side to side, flap-ping his wings and giving the swizzling notes typical of weavers Found in reedbeds, agricultural lands and upland vleis.

ROY JOHANNESSON

Above left: breeding male
Left: female

Southern Masked-Weaver   *Ploceus velatus* 11-14,5 cm

Breeding male   H. VON HORSTEN

Female   W.R. TARBOTON

The breeding male can be distinguished from the male Village Weaver by its *uniform yellowish-green back* and by the *greater extent of black on the head*, especially on the forehead. The non-breeding male, female and imm. are alike, having yellowish underparts and olive-brown upperparts, and are difficult to differentiate from other non-breeding weavers. It is usually found in small breeding colonies; when not breeding it forms part of mixed flocks of bishops and weavers. Occurs in thornveld, trees over water and in agricultural lands.

Lesser Masked-Weaver   *Ploceus intermedius* 13-14 cm

Breeding male   G. CUBITT

Female   J. LAURIE

Slightly smaller and more compact than the similar Southern Masked-Weaver, this species is easily distinguished in breeding plumage by having *more extensive black on the head*, encompassing the crown and extending on to the throat in a *rounded, not pointed bib*. This species further differs from the Southern Masked-Weaver in all plumages by having *a pale, not red eye* and *bluish, not brown legs and feet*. Colonial breeder in trees overhanging rivers and dams, and in reedbeds. Out of the breeding season, it forms mixed flocks with other weavers.

Yellow Weaver   *Ploceus subaureus*   11-14 cm

Breeding male

Female

The male in breeding plumage is best distinguished from the breeding male Cape Weaver by its smaller size, more *vivid golden-yellow plumage*, less extensive wash of orange on the face and a *bright red, not cream eye*. The non-breeding male and the female and imm. are similar in appearance; unlike other weavers in alternate plumage, they have a distinct pale yellow throat and breast which is sharply demarcated from the white underparts. It breeds in reedbeds, but is often seen foraging in woodland.

Red-billed Quelea   *Quelea quelea*   11-13 cm

Breeding male

Non-breeding female

The male of this small finch in breeding plumage is unmistakable with his *black face bordered with red* and his *bright red bill and legs*. The non-breeding male and female are very sparrow-like but still show the red bill and legs. The breeding female has a horn-coloured bill. This species is best known for concentrating in hundreds of thousands of birds which fly in tightly packed flocks. Occurs in mixed dry woodland, grasslands and farmlands.

Southern Red Bishop   *Euplectes orix*   **10-11 cm**

Breeding male   **Female**

A male Southern Red Bishop in breeding plumage can easily be identified by the combination of its *bright orange and black plumage*. The female, imm. and non-breeding male are not easily distinguished from the similarly plumaged Yellow-crowned Bishop but this species appears darker and has more heavily streaked underparts. The male performs a spectacular display fight in which he fluffs out his feathers and, with rapid wing beats, whizzes to and fro like a giant bumblebee. Found in reedbeds adjoining fresh water, and agricultural lands.

Yellow-crowned Bishop   *Euplectes afer*   **9,5-10,5 cm**

Most often seen together with widows and weavers in very large mixed flocks when all the birds appear as unidentifiable 'little brown jobs' with mottled and streaked brown and buff plumages. This species most closely resembles the Southern Red Bishop in this obscure plumage but is noticeably smaller, more compact and is paler overall with reduced streaking on the breast and flanks. The male in breeding plumage is easily identified by his *yellow and black coloration* and his *unusual bumble-bee-like flight* over his territory. Found in reedbeds and grasses near water, and arable crops and grasslands.

**Breeding male above,
female below**

129

Yellow Bishop *Euplectes capensis* 15 cm

Breeding male

Female

The predominantly black plumage of the male widowbirds breeding plumage gives them their name, but all show some diagnostic yellow or red markings. This species has a *bright yellow low rump and lower back* and *a yellow shoulder patch*. The female shows a dull yellow rump which distinguishes her from all other female widowbirds. The male in non-breeding plumage resembles the female but, in flight, shows a yellow rump and shoulder patch. Frequents damp grassy areas, bracken-covered mountain valleys and fynbos.

Fan-tailed Widowbird *Euplectes axillaris* 15-17 cm

Only two widowbirds in the region have red shoulder patches: this species and the Long-tailed Widowbird. This species is far smaller and the breeding male does not have a very long tail. Also, the red shoulder of this species has no broad buff stripe on the lower edge. In non-breeding plumage, the male is easily distinguished by his red shoulder patch but the female lacks any obvious field characters. Occurs over reedbeds, damp grasslands and in sugarcane plantations.

Breeding male

130

White-winged Widowbird   *Euplectes albonotatus* **15-19 cm**

Breeding male

Female

L. HES

W.G. McILLERON

Could possibly be confused with the Yellow Bishop in breeding and non-breeding plumages but this species *lacks any yellow on the back or rump* and the *yellow shoulder patch is bordered by white* on the lower edge. The male in non-breeding plumage retains the yellow and white shoulder patch. The female lacks the dull yellow rump of the female Yellow Bishop. During the non-breeding season, flocks in flight are easily recognized by their diagnostic yellow and white shoulder patches. Found in damp grassy areas and in reedbeds.

Red-collared Widowbird   *Euplectes ardens* **15 + 25 cm tail br.** ♂

Breeding male

Female

N. BRICKELL

N. BRICKELL

The breeding male resembles a diminutive Long-tailed Widowbird and at a distance they might be confused, but this species lacks the red shoulder. At closer range the red crescentic marking on the throat can easily be seen. The non-breeding male, the female and imm. are very similar to the plainly coloured bishops and other widowbirds but this species shows a boldly striped head and plain buffy underparts. It is one of the few species that has adapted to the sugarcane belt in the east of the region.

Long-tailed Widowbird   *Euplectes progne*   ♂ =19 + 40 cm tail; ♀ =1◖

Above: non-breeding
Left: Breeding male

The breeding male is unmistakable with his *exceptionally long◖ tail and bright red shoulder patches bordered with buff*. Out of the breeding season, the tail is lost and the plumage becomes mot◖ tled brown and buff but he retains the red shoulder character◖ The female is the largest of all the female widowbirds, has a rounded wing floppy flight and shows a dark underwing. When displaying, the male flies◖ with the long tail dangling and held spread, and his wings flapping with◖ jerky circular movements. Inhabits open grasslands and damp grassy valleys.

Pin-tailed Whydah   *Vidua macroura*   12 + 22 cm tail br. ♂

Above: male
Below: female

The breeding male is unmistakable with his *pied plumage and very long black tail*. The female and non-breeding male are a *drab, mottled brown and buff with dark stripes on the head* but the male in this plumage still shows a red bill. In this obscure plumage they can be distinguished from the similarly marked bishops by the dark streaks on the buff head and by the white outertail feathers. During the breeding season the male performs a low aerial display flight in which he dances and bobs in front of females. Found in grasslands, and in suburbia.

Shaft-tailed Whydah   *Vidua regia*   **12 + 22 cm tail br. ♂**

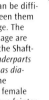

Where the ranges of the Pin-tailed and Shaft-tailed whydah overlap, it can be difficult to distinguish between them in non-breeding plumage. The males in breeding plumage are easily differentiated as the Shaft-tailed has *warm buff underparts and collar and the tail has diagnostic spatulate tips*. The non-breeding male and female are slightly paler and have fainter head markings than the similarly plumaged Pin-tailed Whydah. The male has a bounding and bobbing display flight. Occurs in grassy areas in dry thornveld and broadleafed woodland.

Left: breeding male

Blue Waxbill   *Uraeginthus angolensis*   **13 cm**

Male   **Female**

A small, *pale brownish* waxbill which has a diagnostic *powder blue face and breast*. The female is paler than the male with less blue on the face and underparts. It feeds on the ground; when disturbed it flies into low areas of bush to hide and gives its soft 'weep-weep' call. Usually occurs in pairs or small flocks and in drier areas frequently visits waterholes or livestock drinking troughs. Occurs in dry areas of mixed woodlands and thornveld.

Violet-eared Waxbill   *Granatina granatina* **15 cm**

The most colourful waxbill, the male has a *cinnamon body, iridescent violet ear patches* (diagnostic), *a bright blue rump and red eyes and bill*. The female and imm. are far paler but still show diagnostic violet ear patches and blue rump. Occurs in pairs or small family parties. Secretive, except when it arrives to drink at waterholes and troughs, when it mixes freely with other waxbills and weavers. Frequents dry thornveld, rivercourses and grassy roadsides.

Above: male
Below: female

Bronze Mannikin   *Lonchura cucullata* **9 cm**

Adult

Immature

This *tiny, black-headed bird* is easily identified by its *brown, black and white plumage*. The bronze-green shoulder is not eas⹁ to see unless the bird is in sunlight but the barred brown flank⹁ contrast clearly with the white breast. The imm. is complete⹁ dun brown with a small yellow gape: in this plumage the imm. wou⹁ be accompanied by adults. Small groups are often seen huddled sid⹁ by side on a perch. Found in grassy areas in woodlands, forest edges an⹁ damp regions.

Yellow-fronted Canary   *Serinus mozambicus*   **10-12 cm**

A. WILSON

Where their ranges overlap, the Yellow-fronted Canary could be confused with the male Yellow Canary but this species has a distinct *black line through the eye, a black moustachial stripe* and a grey nape. These features tend to emphasize the yellow around the eye which the Yellow Canary never shows. It is distinguished from the Brimstone Canary by being smaller and by having a less robust bill. The imm. is a more buffy yellow below. Found in thornveld, mixed woodland, forest edge, and in suburbia.

Black-throated Canary   *Serinus atrogularis*   **11 cm**

N. BRICKELL

A small, nondescript grey and brown canary which has a diagnostic *black speckled throat*. It also has a *bright yellow rump* which contrasts with the drab plumage and is conspicuous as the bird takes flight. An active and shy canary, very quick to take flight, it occurs in groups or small flocks. Frequents dry woodland, thornveld and scrub.

Cape Canary   *Serinus canicollis*   11-13 cm

Adult   **Immature**

The lilting, tinkling call note, unlike that of any other canary, is often the first indication of this species' presence. Small groups are usually encountered as they feed on grasses and other seeding plants; when flushed, they show their *grey and green plumage*. It differs from the Yellow-fronted Canary by *lacking that species' facial markings*. The imm. resembles the female Yellow Canary but has yellowish-green, not white streaked underparts. Frequents fynbos and mountainous terrain.

Brimstone Canary   *Serinus sulphuratus*   13-15 cm

This is the *largest of the 'yellow' canaries* and in all plumages it shows a much *heavier, more robust bill*. The dark southern birds can be told from the Yellow and Yellow-fronted canaries by their larger size, chunkier bill and the greenish wash across the breast. The more vivid northern birds are distinguished from the Yellow Canary by the more massive bill and by lacking a contrasting yellow rump. An inconspicuous canary, it occurs in pairs or small groups. Found in scrub, woodlands and coastal scrub.

Yellow Canary *Serinus flaviventris* **13 cm**

Male

Female

The 'yellow' canary of the more arid regions. It has a dark form which might be mistaken for a Brimstone or Yellow-fronted canary but it *lacks the greenish breast band of the former and the black facial markings* of the latter. It is a much *brighter golden-yellow* than the pale form Brimstone Canary. The female and imm. differ from the female Cape Canary by having whitish, not yellowish-green underparts streaked with brown. An inhabitant of Karoo and coastal scrub, thornveld and mountainous scrub.

Golden-breasted Bunting *Emberiza flaviventris* **15-16 cm**

The *black and white striped head, chestnut mantle and yellow-orange breast* are diagnostic in this bunting. The female and imm. are duller versions of the male. It often reveals its presence by giving a nasal, buzzy 'zzhrrrr' call or its song, a varied 'weechee-weechee-weechee', from within the canopy of a tree. Feeds on the ground; when flushed, will fly a short distance, displaying its white outertail, white wing bars and chestnut back. Found in thornveld, broadleafed woodland and exotic plantations.

137

Cape Bunting *Emberiza capensis* **16 cm**

ROY JOHANNESSON

The head pattern of this bird resembles that of the Golden-breasted Bunting but is grey and black striped. This, combined with the grey breast and chestnut shoulder, render it easy to identify. In its rocky and sandy terrain this small bird shuffles around on the ground searching for food; when disturbed, it will dash for cover behind a rock or bush. The call is a nasal, ascending 'zzooo-zeh-zee-zee' and the song, given from a prominent rock, consists of a series of chirping notes.

Lark-like Bunting *Emberiza impetuani* **14 cm**

A WILSON

It is the *lack of any definite field characters* in this *drab and dowdy* bird that points to its identification. It might be mis-taken for a lark but it exhibits typical bunting behaviour, hopping over stones and grubbing around for seeds on bare ground. It is often flushed from road verges. It occurs in the drier areas and commonly frequents waterholes and livestock drinking troughs, sometimes in large numbers. Its contact call is a short 'tuc-tuc'. Found in dry rocky valleys, desert edge and open plains.

BIRDING ETIQUETTE

Once you are equipped with a pair of binoculars, a notebook and a field guide, you are on the road to birding and no other licence is required. Access to most game and nature reserves, wildlife sanctuaries and wilderness areas is allowed if the necessary permits are arranged prior to the visit, and any admission fees paid. Most other birding areas are on privately owned land and, although birding from the road into these areas is acceptable, it is not advisable to go across the veld unless you have sought permission from the landowner. Enter fields through gates or by climbing carefully through and not over a fence.

The ever-increasing number of birders is placing pressure on the better known birding areas and, to avoid being denied access, birders should observe a simple code of etiquette. In their innocent pursuit birders can disturb and harm the very things that have taken their interest. Watching a flock of terns or roosting waders on a beach might seem harmless enough but if you put them to flight you are directly causing a disturbance. This is tolerable if you do it only once, but repeatedly disturbing flocks causes distress and the birds subsequently move away altogether – this often happens if there is more than one birder in the area. Making any kind of close approach to breeding colonies of birds such as weavers, bishops, herons and seabirds can cause incalculable harm and may even result in the entire colony disbanding and deserting, with a total breeding failure in that season. Viewing birds in this situation is simple if a quiet and careful approach is made or, even better, if you use a spotting scope and thus avoid too close an approach altogether.

It is easy to recognize the situations in which birds will flush. They become very agitated, sometimes giving off alarm notes, and will begin wing stretching. Respect these signals and leave the vicinity. General disturbance of any breeding birds should be avoided – with experience you will be able to tell if a bird is holding a territory and actively nesting. A nesting bird or a bird with young may feign injury, give alarm calls, or dive bomb an intruder in an effort to distract attention away from its nest or young. When you recognize these signals it is best to limit your time in the immediate area in case you cause the birds to desert.

A technique which is being employed more frequently is that of using a tape recording of a bird's call or song to entice the bird into the open for better viewing. This practice is useful for attracting the more furtive species and, in particular, nocturnal owls and nightjars. It does not do any harm if done very infrequently but most certainly will if the bird is repeatedly lured to a tape recording. A bird responding to a taped call is doing so to seek out an invader to its territory, and if it cannot see the intruder to chase it away, it will inevitably become confused. If continually lured to a tape, the bird defending its territory will eventually abandon the area.

The key to 'unobtrusive' birding is to have the bird's interests in mind. Remember all the time that the habitat in which you are watching the bird is fragile: take care not to damage it or to disturb the area.

Actively involve yourself in a local or national conservation society and draw their attention to areas near you that need conserving or that are being disturbed or developed. If added up on a national scale, the small areas of natural habitat which are rapidly being destroyed and cleared for development would cover a vast area.

GLOSSARY OF TERMS

Alien A bird which is not indigenous to the area.

Call Short notes given by males and females for alarm and contact purposes (see Song).

Cap Area encompassing the forehead and crown.

Casque A helmet or helmet-like process on the bill.

Cere Coloured bare skin at the base of the upper mandible (in raptors).

Colonial Associating in close proximity, either while roosting, feeding or nesting.

Crest Elongated feathers on the forehead, crown or nape.

Cryptic Pertaining to camouflage coloration.

Decurved Curving downwards.

Display A pattern of behaviour in which the bird attracts attention while it is defending territory or courting a female, for example.

Endemic Restricted to a certain region.

Eye-ring Circle of coloured feathers immediately behind the eye.

Feral Species that have escaped from captivity and now live in the wild.

Flush To rouse and put to flight.

Immature A bird that has moulted its juvenile plumage but has not yet attained full adult plumage.

Juvenile The first full-feathered plumage of a young bird.

Migrant A species that undertakes long-distance flights between its wintering and breeding areas.

Moustachial stripes Lines running from the base of the bill to the sides of the throat (see malar region in illustration).

Parasitize When a bird lays its eggs in the nest of another species for the purposes of incubation.

Plumage Feathering of a kind.

Primaries The outermost major flight feathers of the wing.

Resident A bird that occurs throughout the year in a region and is not known to undertake migration.

Roost To sleep or rest, either in flocks or singly.

Secondaries Flight feathers of the wing, adjoining the primary feathers.

Shield Bare patch of skin at the base of the bill and on the forehead. Often brightly coloured.

Song A series of notes given by the male to proclaim his territory (see Call).

Summer visitor A bird that is absent from the region during winter.

Territory An area that a bird establishes and subsequently defends from others.

Vent Area from the belly to the undertail coverts.

PARTS OF A BIRD

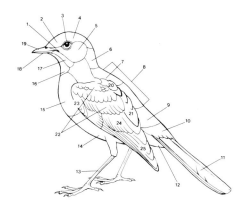

1 lores	10 uppertail coverts	19 upper mandible
2 forehead	11 tail	20 scapulars
3 eye-ring	12 undertail coverts	21 tertials
4 crown	13 tarsus	22 wing coverts
5 ear coverts	14 belly	23 alula
6 nape	15 breast	24 secondaries
7 mantle	16 throat	25 primaries
8 back	17 malar region	
9 rump	18 lower mandible	

HABITAT

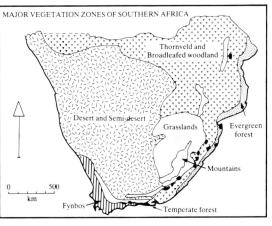

MAJOR VEGETATION ZONES OF SOUTHERN AFRICA

Thornveld and Broadleafed woodland

Desert and Semi-desert

Grasslands

Evergreen forest

Mountains

0   500
km

Fynbos

Temperate forest

The map of the region (above) shows the major vegetation zones mentioned in the text. Bird distribution is contained by, and in many cases, restricted to specialized habitats within these zones.

FURTHER READING

The following books may be of interest to those wishing to learn more about birds and bird-watching.

Berruti, A., and Sinclair, J.C. 1983. *Where to Watch Birds in Southern Africa*. Struik Publishers, Cape Town.

Ginn, P., McIlleron, W.G., and Milstein, P. 1989. *The Complete Book of Southern African Birds*. Struik Winchester, Cape Town.

Harrison, P. 1983. Seabirds: *An Identification Guide*. Croom Helm, London.Heinzel, H., Fitter, R., and Parslow, J. 1972. *The Birds of Britain and Europe with North Africa and the Middle East*. Collins, London

King, B., Woodcock, M., and Dickinson, E.C. 1974. *A Field Guide to the Birds of South East Asia*. Collins, London.

Maclean, G.L. 1984 (5th edition). Roberts' *Birds of Southern Africa*. The Trustees of the John Voelcker Bird Book Fund, Cape Town.

Maclean, G.L. 1993. Roberts' *Birds of Southern Africa*. John Voelcker Bird Book Fund, Cape Town.

Newman, K.B. 1987. *Birds of the Kruger National Park*. Southern Book Publishers, Johannesburg.

Newman, K.B. 1983. *Newman's Birds of Southern Africa*. Macmillan South Africa, Johannesburg.

Pickford, P. and B., and Tarboton, W. 1989. *Southern African Birds of Prey*. Struik Publishers, Cape Town.

Robbins, C.S., Bruun, B., and Zimm, H.S. 1966. *A Guide to the Field Identification: Birds of North America*. Golden Press, New York.

Sinclair, I., and Goode, D. 1986. *Struik Pocket Guide Series: Birds of Prey*. Struik Publishers, Cape Town.

Sinclair, I., and Goode, D. 1987. *Struik Pocket Guide Series: Highveld Birds*. Struik Publishers, Cape Town.

Sinclair, I., Meakin, P., and Goode, D. 1990. *Struik Pocket Guide Series: Common Birds*. Struik Publishers, Cape Town.

Sinclair, I., Whyte, I. 1991. *Field Guide to Birds of the Kruger National Park*. Struik Publishers, Cape Town.

Sinclair, I. 1994. *Field Guide to the Birds of southern Africa*. Struik Publishers, Cape Town.

Sinclair, I. 1995. *Southern African Birds: A photographic guide*. Struik Publishers, Cape Town.

Sinclair, I., and Mendelsohn, J.M. 2001. *Everyone's Guide to South African Birds*. Struik Publishers, Cape Town.

Sinclair, I., and Sinclair, J. 1995. *Birds of Namibia*. Struik Publishers, Cape Town.

Sinclair, I., Hockey, P, and Tarboton, W. 2002. *Sasol Field Guide to Southern African Birds*. Struik Publishers, Cape Town.

Sinclair, I., and Ryan, P. 2003. *Field Guide to Birds of Africa*. Struik Publishers, Cape Town.

Sinclair, J.C., Mendelsohn, J.M., and Johnson, P. 1981. *Everyone's Guide to South African Birds*. CNA, Johannesburg.

Steyn, P. 1982. *Birds of Prey of Southern Africa*. David Philip, Cape Town.

INDEX